Nevis

Nevis

Queen of the Caribbees
FIFTH EDITION

Joyce Gordon

MACMILLAN
CARIBBEAN

Macmillan Education

Between Towns Road, Oxford OX4 3PP
A division of Macmillan Publishers Limited
Companies and representatives throughout the world
www.macmillan-caribbean.com

ISBN 1-4050-3008-9

First published 1985
This fifth edition published 2005

Designed by Amanda Easter Design Ltd.
Maps by Tech Type
Cover design by Gary Fielder, AC Design
Cover photographs by Donald Nausbaum

The author and publishers would like to thank the following for
permisssion to reproduce their photographs: Michael Bourne
p 8; Andrew Gordon pp 14/15, 55 (bottom); Chris Huxley pp 4,
31 (top), 60, 67 (top), 68; Donald Nausbaum: all other photos

Printed and bound in Thailand
2009 2008 2008 2006 2005
10 9 8 7 6 5 4 3 2 1

Contents

Acknowledgements

I would like to acknowledge my gratitude to the many people of Nevis who have helped me to write this book. It is not possible to name everyone but I would particularly like to thank the Deputy Governor-General, Mr Paris and the Right Honourable Arthur Evelyn, Civil Servants from various departments, and friends, such as the Byrons, the Maynards and the late Eva Wilkins. The Ven. Archdeacon Blant, Canon G Walker from St Kitts and the Revd. Ghum of the Nevis Methodist Church were all most generous with their assistance, as were Mr Howell of Cane Garden and the Staff of Zetlands Plantation Inn. Sheila Nehlsen and Margaret Lyman made available copies of historical documents. In the Museum of Nevis History the Robinsons have kindly given me access to the Archives and library and Mrs Epps and Mrs Paddock helped me find relevant material. Quentin Henderson has provided the information on beekeeping. I am especially grateful for the use of all the books belonging to Mr R. Abrahams from his Nelson Collection, as well as books lent to me by Mrs Polly Wilson and others.

Our thanks go the Nevis Philatelic Bureau for permission to reproduce the Nevis stamps.

I am greatly indebted to Adelma Walters who did so much of the typing, as well as Christine Lupinacci and Karin Little.

Lastly this book is dedicated to my husband Ian, who gave me every encouragement and endless help, as well as to Andrew, who has photographed Nevis as it is today.

Joyce Gordon 1985

I would also like to thank the people who helped me with the fifth edition of this book. I am most grateful to Augustine Merchant, Arthur Evelyn, Miriam Knorr, Joan and David Robinson, Barbara and Ted Cox, Maureen Labinski, Lornette Hanley, Captain Arthur Anslyn, and the Lupinacci familly.

2005

Foreword

I am pleased to have been asked to write the foreword for this handbook on Nevis.

Firstly, I should compliment the author for this concise yet comprehensive production of vital and invaluable information relating to the natural and historic heritage of the island and its unique charm and beauty.

The Ministry of Tourism welcomes this publication not only as a guidebook for visitors, but also as a reliable source of information pertaining to the social and cultural aspects of Nevis.

I therefore recommend this book to the researcher, taxi driver, student and all other Nevisians who wish to know more about the island which was once considered as being the 'Queen of the Caribbean'.

Honourable A. L. Evelyn J.P.
The Minister of Tourism (1985)
(Nevis Island Administration)

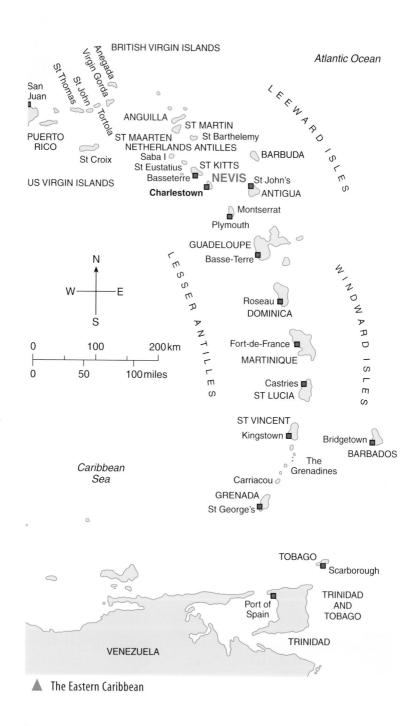

The Eastern Caribbean

Introduction

This book is about an island situated in the north-eastern part of the Caribbean, 17° 15' north, 62° 40' west. It is an island of great beauty, which has known fame and experienced tragedies. Coconuts grow along the seashore, its mountain is covered with forest. Best clothes are worn for church on Sundays, and everyone knows about cricket. Mangoes hang from the trees in summer time and breadfruit grow in every ghaut. Its mountain is often capped with mist or cloud. It is called Nevis. There are only 36 square miles (93 sq.km) of Nevis and it is separated from the neighbouring island of St Kitts by a channel barely two miles wide. The climate is tropical and maritime with the trade winds blowing from an easterly direction most of the year. The temperature never falls below 15°C nor rises above 35°C, with little difference between winter and summer.

The first part of this book is a brief history of Nevis from 1628 when it became one of the first English colonies, until 1983, when together with St Kitts it became an independent state. The second part of the book is about the island as it is today: a guide for the visitor who can discover the charm and delights of this very special island.

▲ Nelson Spring, Cotton Ground

❶ Historical background

It is said that in 1493, when Columbus sighted this island with the mountain capped with mist and cloud, he named it 'Nuestro Senora de las Nieves' (our Lady of the Snows) and that the name Nevis slowly evolved from that. Columbus was then on his second voyage, in search of a new route to Asia and the Indies. This island was never colonised by the Spanish but was regarded as Spain's by right of discovery. It was Columbus who called the islands he discovered in the Caribbean the 'West Indies'.

Nevis was colonised through St Kitts in 1628. Thomas Warner had arrived there in 1623 and, when he returned to England in 1625, King Charles I granted him the first Royal Commission for the Isle of St Christopher, the Isle of Nevis, the Isle of Barbados and the Isle of Montserrat. In 1628 Captain Anthony Hilton was appointed the first Governor of Nevis by Thomas Warner; thus the two islands were among the first English colonies. By 1644 the islands were transferred from the proprietary system to the protection of the English Crown, whose representative was the Governor-General of the Leeward Isles. He was responsible for defence, the enforcement of the Navigation Acts and colonial rules, and the collection of taxes owing to the Crown. The Nevis Council and Assembly made local laws which were subject to Royal assent. Nevis had become part of the British Empire of the Americas.

Extracts from the Acts of Assembly passed in the early years of the colony:

1664 *An export duty of $4^1/2\%$ to be paid on every commodity of the island.*
A rent of 201 lbs of tobacco to be paid per pole of land.

1680 *Act to prevent the landing of infected persons from ships; penalty for landing persons without a licence: 10 000 lbs of sugar.*

1698 *Act to regulate prices of fresh provisions: beef, mutton, pork, fresh turtle, goat $-6^1/2$d per lb. Salted beef, etc – 4d per lb. Only to be sold in Charlestown market.*

1698 *Act regarding Assembly men: if chosen to serve must comply; those who refused to serve to pay for every such offence £20 current money of the island.*

1699 *Act against slaves running away with boats or canoes: if apprehended to be sent to gaol, judged as felons and to suffer the pains of death without benefit of the clergy.*

1700 *Act for suppressing thatch houses: ' ... forasmuch as many sudden and dreadful fires have happened in the several towns of this island...'*

1701 *Act to prevent Papists and reputed Papists from settling on the island in the future; those already settled to be sent off the island if so ordered.*

1701 *Physicians and surgeons not allowed to practise without a licence or taking of oaths.*

1701 *Act for earlier repair of the highways; two people from each precinct to survey the highways each December 2nd, and to mend them twice yearly in July and December.*

1704 *Act for making Indian Castle a shipping place, to ship off all sugar, cotton, indigo and other goods from there to Charlestown where 4½% duty to be paid: ' ... because in the Parish of St George the lands remain unmanured ... and the inhabitants have left that part of the island because of no shipping place.'*

1711 *Act to establish Courts of the Queens Bench and to settle due methods for the administration of justice in the islands.*

1721 *Act for raising a Poll Tax on all slaves and negroes as well as on freeholders, householders and traders of the island.*

The first English settlers who came to Nevis wanted to acquire cheap land, or were perhaps seeking a life in the unknown, having heard stories of the great riches found in the Americas. Mainly it was people from the lower and middle classes who came: craftsmen hoping their skills would be in demand, carpenters, blacksmiths, masons, tailors and people with farming interests. Poorer immigrants came as bonded and indentured servants. In return for a free passage they signed an agreement to work for five years receiving 17s 6d each year plus food and a home (those with a craft received £25). At the termination of their bonded service they were given five acres of land to farm on their own. Several thousands of such people came to St Kitts between 1629 and 1643 and from there went on to Nevis. These colonists had a lot to contend with. Land had to be cleared, for trees then covered much of the island; the stones which had to be moved were used for buildings and roads. There were wild pigs and iguanas on the island. Because they were a source of meat they were extensively slaughtered until both were exterminated. Boats were made from hollowed-out tree trunks and used to catch turtles and fish. The initial journey of the newcomers took at least six weeks and was uncomfortable and hazardous; many suffered from the ill effects of the journey only to find that on arrival they had to acclimatise to the heat as well as facing endemic diseases such as yellow fever and malaria.

Slowly the colony was established. The first town was Jamestown, situated on the leeward side of the island and named after the reigning monarch. Charlestown was built after 1660. It became the principal town and port after Jamestown was damaged by a tidal wave in 1680. (Recent research shows that Jamestown was not totally destroyed and was referred to in official documents as late as 1807 and in baptismal records in 1877.) The population in 1650 was estimated to be 5000. Tobacco crops, as well as spices and indigo, were grown and exported to England in return for imports. The currency was 'bundles of dried tobacco leaves' and later sugar. The *Navigation Acts*, which were passed in 1651 and 1660, meant that only English ships could carry goods to the West Indies and a heavy customs rate was charged on all imports. Not all of these early settlers found the life congenial. Some were very poor and the island was considered to be overcrowded. Two thousand people left in 1655 to attempt to settle in Jamaica and others moved to the American continent. Tobacco was losing favour, for the Virginian settlers were producing far better crops; sugar was already being produced in places such as Barbados and Antigua. For the next two hundred years everything connected with sugar dominated the history of this island.

The development of the sugar plantations depended entirely on slave labour. Although the price of land had risen by 10% in the 1670s, the capital invested in slaves was the major part of the planters' investment. White labour, bonded and indentured servants were unsuitable and unwilling to hoe and crush the cane. They and the poorer farmers who remained on the island became absorbed into the plantations, working as clerks and storekeepers, or they became tradespeople. The negro labourers worked in the cane fields, the mills and the sugar factories; others were domestic servants. Some were trained to be craftsmen and constructed the roads and buildings. In 1716 the price of a slave was £80. The routine and customs of plantation life determined the whole existence of the slaves; a Slave Code, dated 1717, with subsequent amendments, laid down all the rules to control them. Their treatment depended entirely on the attitude of their masters; good and bad years of the sugar crop affected the well being of every slave. In 1788 four hundred died of starvation following a total crop failure the previous year.

▲ House near Newcastle

Nevis was a market for selling slaves to neighbouring islands when the Royal African Company had the monopoly in providing slaves from 1660 to 1698. The number of slaves increased from 3849 in 1678 to 10 000 in 1778, whilst at the same time the proportion of black to white people increased from equal proportions to ten black to one white. Large gatherings and meetings were forbidden to prevent rioting. The market was the only occasion when slaves from the different plantations could meet and there they sold surplus produce from their small parcels of land. Although the identity of the African, such as his name, his tribe, his language and his religion was lost, some of his African culture did remain. Singing and dancing emerged as Caribbean jump-ups, masqueraders and calypsos; their musical instruments also survived. Obeahism and Myalism were cults which were kept alive; the knowledge the Myal men had of curing sickness by using herbs and plants has been handed down to generations of Nevisians.

In 1826 Henry Coleridge visited Nevis with his brother Bishop Coleridge, who was the first Bishop of Barbados. Charlestown he thought was a larger, smarter and more populous place than the capital of Montserrat; the Court House was a handsome building.

He was made extremely uncomfortable during the night he spent at Government House by the mosquitoes which pestered him unmercifully. He praised the delicious fruits the island produced and considered the oranges here and from St Kitts the finest in the West Indies. Mr Cottle had offered him strawberries and peaches and wondered why other fruits which grew in more temperate climates could not be grown here. He referred to the depression of the sugar market and noted there were already two steam engines grinding canes which he had not seen anywhere else except in Trinidad. He suggested that the additional revenue might make it worthwhile for other estates to invest in steam power. This would save much labour which could then be used in growing more provisions of different sorts. He also thought the planters ought to be more attentive to the clothing of their slaves; domestics ought to wear shoes and women field-workers ought not to be bare-bosomed. He rode around the island in a gig which he considered to be a sign of civilisation, and found the roads tolerable, and the 'island rich and verdant ... perfectly cultivated and enlivened with old planters' houses of a superior style'.

In 1833 the British Parliament passed a law (the *Emancipation Act*) to free all slaves in the British colonies after a six-year apprenticeship and with compensation to the owners. Emancipation was to come into effect on 1 August 1834. The first Monday in August is still celebrated as an annual holiday. In Nevis, a total of 7225 slaves were emancipated; 4636 had been field-workers and 1207 domestic slaves. There were 399 claims for compensation from the British Government. Forty estates had over 100 slaves, sixty estates had between 11 and 100 and over two hundred estates owned fewer than 10 slaves. Black people had the same rights as white and every freed slave acquired a surname which in most cases was taken from his previous master's; in church registers the newly converted were no longer described as 'slave'; now their craft or trade was attached to their name, such as carpenter, cooper, saddler, domestic. People built their homes away from the plantations. They moved to the ghauts and to land where they could grow more food for themselves and take the surplus to markets. Hucksters came into being, traders who worked for a small margin of profit selling goods around the island. Market day was changed to Saturday after more people were baptised by the Anglican and Methodist churches. The colonial power which had the duty to finance schools gave money to the churches for the provision of new schools.

Nevis underwent many changes during the next century. Administration became the responsibility of the Crown. The

Council and Assembly were merged into one chamber in 1866 with half of its ten members being nominated and half elected. The Federal Colony of the Leeward Isles was constituted in 1871, Nevis being a member until 1882 when it ceased to be a single unit with its own legislature and was united with St Kitts. Economic conditions deteriorated during this time and by 1890 an air of gentle decay was settling over the whole island. Charlestown was described as a 'sleepy place with many of its buildings locked from day to day and emptied of its folk'. Emigration began as early as 1840. Trinidad attracted the first migrants who found they could get higher wages for field-work than they received in Nevis. Later in the century migration to the United States started; the goldfields in Venezuela attracted a few and others went to work in Panama where for thirty years immigrants helped to build the canal. Those who survived the appalling conditions were known as the 'mosquito conquerors'. Those who remained in Nevis were reluctant to be employed; more people worked their own land. Share-cropping was introduced on estates where cotton was grown. Returning immigrants used their capital to buy up estates or became owners of shops and businesses. Remittances sent by relatives working overseas played an important part in supporting the less fortunate families and dependants.

The Great World War of 1914–1918 brought a temporary improvement to the economy. The price for cotton rose and sugar was sold for £100 per ton in England (owing to the drastic state of the European sugar industry). In 1929 there were 3000 acres of cotton and 3000 acres of sugar being cultivated. One third of the island's inhabitants were employed in agriculture and a third of the population of approximately 12 000 were illiterate. The economic conditions were worsened by the world depression of the 1930s; cotton was no longer in demand by mills in Lancashire which suffered a severe slump; neither Europe nor America had any desire to invest money in Nevis and the island suffered great hardships as the economy continued to decline. In one hundred years the average agricultural wage had only increased from 6d to 1s 6d. Subsistence farming continued and the Government bought up several estates for as little as £3 per acre in an effort to foster land settlement schemes. It has been said that between the years 1945 and 1965 more was done to improve the condition of life on the island than since emancipation. This was the outcome of the Moyne Commission which had been appointed in 1938 to examine the social and economic conditions in the whole of the West Indies (Lord Moyne was accompanied by Lady Churchill when he visited Nevis). Malaria eradication was one of the important improvements. Better educational facilities were also provided. The introduction of adult suffrage in 1951 was also the result of the Moyne Commission's recommendations. This opened the way to a political awareness and the desire for self-government among the new voters.

▲ Memorial Square, Charlestown

Before completing this historical summary mention must be made of some of the natural disasters and tragedies which have occurred in Nevis. 1772 was known as the year of the great hurricane. On 8 February 1843 an earthquake did irreparable damage to Charlestown. The Court House and many of the houses and stores were levelled, rocks toppled down the mountain-side and estates were devastated. The population was said to have been decimated by epidemics of Asiatic cholera in 1853 and 1854. Hurricanes occurred in 1899 and in 1924 when over £7000 worth of damage to private property was caused as well as £2000 worth to public buildings. Hurricane Hugo which battered the island on 17 September 1989 was said to have been even more ferocious, causing extensive damage to homes, hotels, buildings, power and telephone lines, to vegetation and to the beaches. The greatest tragedy which affected the island's community was when the MV *Christena* sank between St Kitts and Nevis carrying Nevisians home for the August weekend in 1970. The sea was not rough but the boat was overcrowded. More than two hundred people were drowned and, although rescue operations were attempted, only a few survived. There was not a family or community that was not touched by this fatal incident; the whole island mourned. Highly respected professional people, and civil servants as well as hucksters who had been trading their vegetables in Basseterre, all were irreplaceable to the community. Two relief funds were opened to help those in most need; $88 000 was administered by Archdeacon Blant from Nevis, but neither fund compensated for the dreadful catastrophe.

In 1967 more constitutional changes took place when St Kitts-Nevis became an Associated State of the United Kingdom. (Anguilla was also included but seceded three months later.) They were fully self-governing in every aspect except for defence and external affairs. However, full independence was the eventual aim of the two islands. This was duly established under a new constitution on 3 September 1983, thus ending 360 years of colonial rule.

St Kitts-Nevis is a member of the Commonwealth and of the United Nations. The independent nation has its own flag. The Prime Minister of St Kitts-Nevis is head of the Government and rules through his Cabinet and the House of Assembly, which has a Speaker and nine freely elected members plus three nominated members. Her Majesty's representative is the Governor-General on St Kitts and the Deputy Governor-General on Nevis. The Constitution protects the Nevis minority which is guaranteed a third representation in the central Government and has the right

to secede if two-thirds of Nevisians vote to do so. Nevis once more has its own Premier and Assembly of five elected members and a nominated President; the two islands share joint Government finance and administration whilst Nevis controls its own affairs. People returned here from far and wide to participate in the Independence celebrations. There was great jubilation and dancing in Charlestown's main street until dawn; calypsos were sung, youth paraded, choirs sang and bands played. HRH Princess Margaret was welcomed and Cicely Tyson, a film star of Nevisian ancestry, was feted. Fireworks were set alight, parties were given and a Thanksgiving Service was held. It was the beginning of a new era in the history of Nevis.

◀ The flag of Nevis flies over the old Bath Hotel

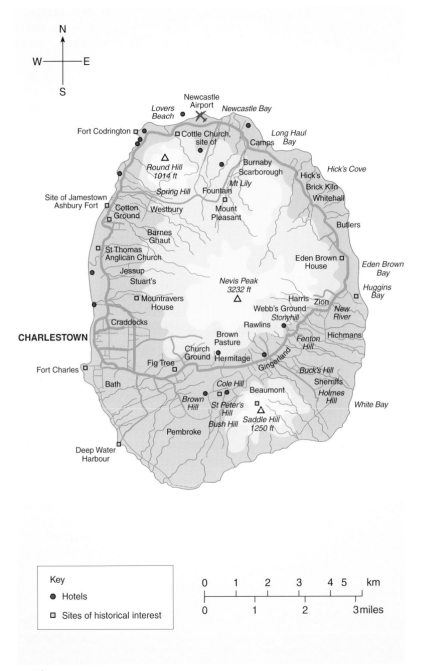

N

W — E

S

Newcastle
Airport
Lovers   Newcastle Bay
Beach
Fort Codrington   Cottle Church,   Long Haul
site of   Camps   Bay
Round Hill   Burnaby   Hick's Cove
1014 ft   Scarborough   Hick's
Mt Lily   Brick Kiln
Spring Hill   Fountain   Whitehall
Site of Jamestown   Westbury   Mount   Butlers
Ashbury Fort   Cotton   Pleasant
Ground
Barnes
Ghaut
St Thomas   Eden Brown   Eden Brown
Anglican Church   House   Bay
Jessup   Nevis Peak   Huggins
Stuart's   3232 ft   Bay
Mountravers   Harris   Zion
House   Webb's Ground   New
Craddocks   Stonyhill   River
Rawlins   Hichmans
CHARLESTOWN   Brown   Fenton
Pasture   Hill
Church   Hermitage   Buck's Hill
Fort Charles   Ground   Sherrifs
Fig Tree   Holmes
Bath   Cole Hill   Beaumont   Hill   White Bay
Brown   St Peter's
Hill   Hill   Saddle Hill
Bush Hill   1250 ft
Pembroke
Deep Water
Harbour

Key

● Hotels

□ Sites of historical interest

| 0 | 1 | 2 | 3 | 4 5 | km |
| 0 | | 1 | | 2 | 3 miles |

▲ Nevis

9

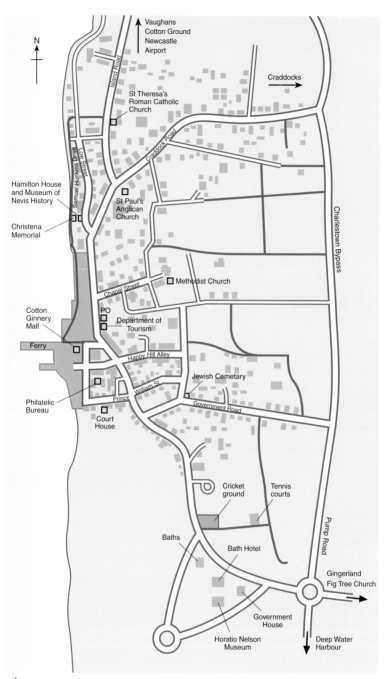

N

Vaughans
Cotton Ground
Newcastle
Airport

Island Road

Craddocks →

St Theresa's
Roman Catholic
Church

Craddock Road

Samuel Hunkins Drive

Low Street

Charlestown Bypass

Hamilton House
and Museum of
Nevis History

Christena
Memorial

St Paul's
Anglican
Church

Methodist Church

Chapel Street

Cotton
Ginnery
Mall

PO

Department of
Tourism

Ferry

Happy Hill Alley

Jewish Cemetary

Philatelic
Bureau

William St

Prince

Government Road

Court
House

Cricket
ground

Tennis
courts

Pump Road

Baths

Bath Hotel

Gingerland
Fig Tree Church

Government
House

Deep Water
Harbour

Horatio Nelson
Museum

▲ Charlestown

10

❷ Charlestown

At the beginning of the last century Charlestown was described as a town of departed glories. Now its glories have returned and it has become one of the most attractive towns in the Caribbean. It is best seen by anyone who has time to wander round its streets and along the sea front. The Samuel Hunkins Drive extends from Gallows Bay to the north of the town. All along here there is an extensive view of St Kitts and one can watch the ferries arriving, yachtsmen coming ashore or the cruise ships disgorging their passengers for tours around the island. All freight and heavy goods are now off-loaded in the deep water harbour which lies a few miles south of Charlestown and has a separate road leading from it, thus preventing heavy traffic from coming through the town.

▲ Charlestown

In Main Street there are many examples of West Indian houses built during the nineteenth century providing a residence above and commercial premises below. Longstone House was built around 1830 of local stone and it had a courtyard at the back. The Williams' grocery store has an attractive balustraded balcony providing shade for pedestrians. Many old as well as some of the newly constructed shops and offices have different gingerbread awnings which add charm to the town. The building that now houses the Tourist Office and the Post Office has been restored with great care and sensitivity. It was originally the Customs House and then the Treasury. The Court House was built to replace the original building which was destroyed by fire in 1873. The law courts are held here and the library is housed above. Further along the street is a spacious mansion fronted by a long flight of steps leading to the residence, with space below which originally housed carriages. It was built in 1823 on what was then the outskirts of the town and has withstood hurricanes and earthquakes ever since. It is well worth a stroll up the side streets such as Prince William Street, Happy Hill Alley and especially Chapel Street with the imposing Methodist Chapel at the top and the nineteenth-century manse which adjoins it. Independence Park was once a cemetery built to house the victims of a cholera epidemic who died in 1853. This lies to the north of the town on the main island road.

▲ Court House (first floor) and Library (second floor), Charlestown

There are plenty of shops and boutiques, several small supermarkets and stores of every description. The market where farmers sell their vegetables and fruits is open most days of the week. The old cotton ginnery is now a small shopping mall with a restaurant above.

In the square in front of the Court House there is a memorial to the men of St Kitts and Nevis who died in the two world wars. A simple and moving service is held here every year. On the Samuel Hunkins Drive, outside the Alexander Hamilton House, a memorial has been built in memory of the many people who died when the *Christena* sank. It is mounted on opal matrix stone which was found on Saddle Hill.

It is always hot in Charlestown, and there is always someone to greet you and wish you a good day.

▲ Charlestown

The remains of the Great House at Eden Brown Estate in 1983

3 The Great Houses and their owners

Only the ruins remain of a few Great Houses. Many of them have crumbled away, destroyed by hurricane or fire or abandoned by impoverished owners. In the days of the plantocracy, when sugar was king on the island, there were several very elegant houses built regardless of cost. The remains of the Great House at Eden Brown still convey an impression of its former glory with a view straight out to sea and overlooking the estate, the mill and sugar factory. It was built entirely of stone, unlike some of the earlier wooden houses. The basement was used for storage and as a shelter when storms or hurricanes occurred. The living quarters were on the first floor with a verandah running the length of the house. The bedrooms were also on this floor, situated at each corner for maximum coolness. The cooking took place in an adjoining building. The house contained porticoes and had polished wooden floors as well as carved woodwork. The imposing steps were built in such a way that friends arriving in their carriages had only to mount them in order to reach the front door. It was built at the end of the eighteenth century for a Mr Browne who named it Browne-Eden. A tombstone near the old stable covers the grave of Edward Huggins junior, who married Jane Juxon from St Kitts in 1812 and who was living there when he was killed in a duel by Walter Maynard in 1822. Legal documents dated 1841 reveal that George Juxon Huggins (born 1821) of Browne-Eden had entered into a marriage contract with Caroline Jane Beard of St Kitts. The wedding was to take place the following year and, 'in consideration of the said marriage ...' the father of the bride, Anthony Beard, and two other planters from St Kitts were made trustees of the estate for the benefit of George Huggins and his wife, who were to receive the income from the estate for life. There are conflicting versions of a legend which purports that a certain bridegroom from Eden Brown (which it is now called), on the very eve of his wedding, with the feast prepared and even the table laid, was involved in a duel with his best man following an argument over a maiden. Both men were mortally wounded in the duel, leaving the bride distraught and demented and the Great House abandoned for ever! It is difficult to ascertain how much is fact and how much is fiction in this tragic tale. Was George Juxon Huggins the much lamented bridegroom and what happened to the bride? It is a fact that Mrs Huggins (a widow) owned Eden Brown in 1861 so perhaps the wedding did take place after all. Early in the twentieth century the Great House was lived in by members of the Evelyn family and sugar and cotton were grown on the estate until the 1950s, when it was bought by the Government. The house has fallen into a sad state of disrepair over the past decades and some of the stone work was removed to build the police station and health clinic in Gingerland.

Montravers was a magnificent mansion, three storeys high with vast windows and dramatic arches, in a superb situation, surrounded by a moat. The kitchens were built alongside the main house so that the whole building was L-shaped. It had a ballroom and a staircase wide enough for three ladies in panniered dresses to descend together. The house was built in the early nineteenth century but the original estate was owned and developed by the Pinney family and was one of the most important on the island. John Pretor Pinney, although a prudent, cautious and meticulous person, was rash enough to import four camels in 1778. Their stables still remain, and an attempt was made to convert them into residential quarters. In 1808 Edward Huggins paid £35 650 for the 270-acre estate (he paid for it in ten annual instalments) and his descendants occupied Montravers until the end of the nineteenth century. Mr Grubb-Ewing then became the owner; he abandoned sugar production to plant coconuts on 210 acres. Mr Mills (with his wife Maude Maynard Mills) acted as attorney (manager) and lived in the Great House until it was sold in the 1930s. Until that date it contained a great wealth of Sheraton and Chippendale furniture, beautiful china and an Adam fireplace as well as antique mirrors of large dimensions. The rough path that now leads to this relic of bygone days bears little resemblance to the tree-lined avenue that once had horse-drawn carriages climbing up it to this truly Great House.

Hermitage House is said to be the oldest house on the island. Built around 1680 or earlier, it is an example of a plantation house built of hardwood in a cruciform shape with two small staircases offering easy access for nocturnal wanderings. Nisbet Plantation Inn is the reconstructed plantation house of the Nisbet family. Close by are the remains of the old mill with the date 1778 and the family initials carved in the keystone. Not far from the road from Camps to Mount Lily and hidden deep in the thick vegetation are the remains of yet another substantially built Great House, Mount Pleasant, which has remarkable stone work. At one time this estate was owned by Mr William Mills of Richmond, England, who sold it to Walter Nisbet of Nevis in 1779. At old Manor Hotel the ruins of the Great House still remain, together with the old kitchens, the steam-powered factory and the old 'birthing' room. It is very probable that this room was used as a hospital to ensure the safe delivery of infants born to slaves after the Abolition of Slavery in 1806 when slaves could no longer be brought into the British Colonies. The initials *EH* and the date *1815* are inscribed on the keystone of the main door at Golden Rock Hotel where the original kitchen forms part of the bar and lounge. Edward Huggins' initials also appear on the buildings at Coconut Walk; here the framework of old buildings can be seen black and stark against the mountain in the background.

Nevis attracted several notable families who were less inclined to be absentee owners than those on neighbouring islands. Families such as the Russells and the Herberts were both pro-Royalist and came out during the Commonwealth period, as did the Stapletons. The Herberts owned Montpelier estate for at least three generations covering over a hundred years. John Herbert was President of Nevis for twenty-five years; in 1780 'their stock of negroes were valued at £6000 and he sends annually to England 500 casks of sugar' wrote Horatio Nelson before his marriage to Mr Herbert's niece. Members of the Scottish aristocratic family the Cambuskeith Hamiltons developed a plantation above Charlestown. From their Great House they could see every field of sugar cane. Azariah Pinney arrived in 1685 with a Bible and £15. He started as a trader selling lace which was shipped out to him from his relatives in Dorset, England on the regular cargo ships. He slowly accumulated wealth, became a general merchant, bought houses in Charlestown and finally bought a plantation. He was elected to the House of Assembly and was the Treasurer of Nevis as well as the collector of liquor taxes. The Maynard family came to Nevis from Essex, England at the end of the seventeenth century; at one time Maynards owned several estates including Butlers, Powells, Vervain, Dunbars and New River. They married into other planter families such as the Daniels, Pembertons, Evelyns, Scarboroughs, Mills, etc.

It was considered that life for the plantocracy was pleasant and in most aspects agreeable. Once a plantation had been established an annual routine was followed, fortunes were rarely made and frequently lost. The planters held posts such as Justices of the Peace, Commissioners of Law, councillors, members of the Assembly, vestry men and churchwardens; most of the men served in the island's militia. Great importance was attached to the parties at Government House and the sumptuous balls given by wealthy families. The public treasury paid the entertainment bills of the visiting Governor-General. When Prince William came in 1787, £800 was voted for the festivities; a hundred men sat down to dinner and seventy ladies were at the ball. Prince William Street in Charlestown commemorates this royal visit. The favourite pastime of the men seems to have been drinking rum; if they did not drink themselves to death they ended up with gout! Various crimes of passion were said to have taken place: duels were fought most frequently over money matters or occasionally a wife's infidelity, such as when a Mr Higgins shot his wife's lover.

Women seem to have lived narrow lives and to have been

unenterprising. They took little interest in the plantation work or in the sugar factory and left the daily management of domestic affairs to the negro staff. Their clothes were sent out from England, and the fashionable ladies wore muslin, painted gauzes and light taffetas. Most of the time during the hot summer months was spent indoors. A creole lady would never undertake a walk and protected her skin against the tropical sun by wearing a mask, which resulted in a stewed look. Children, especially the sons, were sent back to England to be educated; thus there was a constant link with the mother country.

But life was not all sunshine and sugar for the planters, who had to contend with hazards such as hurricanes, droughts and infestations of pests. There was no system of hurricane warnings and hurricanes seem to have been as frequent as they are today.

Some estates used steam- or animal-powered mills but on those estates which only used windmills, when there was no wind to work the sails of the mills, the canes rotted in the fields. Sickness and deaths from malaria and yellow fever occurred in all families. A recurring problem for many plantation owners was finance for the purchase of goods as well as for working capital. Debts were common and sugar was used as the main currency on the island. It was easier to accumulate wealth by lending money than by owning a sugar plantation. Throughout the eighteenth century there was the constant threat of French invaders. Above all there was the need to maintain strict discipline on the estates. With the landowners in a minority it is reasonable to assume that fear of revolt was often in the minds of this elite society; they were the enviable 'nouveau riche' of the British Empire.

▲ Hermitage

4 Sugar mills and sugar production

Once there were forty-one windmills working on the island as well as twenty steam-powered mills and twenty-two animal mills. Now many of the mills are only ruins; some have been converted into homes. Cattle mills were the first mills to be built using animals as the source of power to turn the rollers which crushed the cane. Mules and oxen were used yoked to a pole which turned the roller as the animal walked around a wide circle. Windmills replaced cattle mills on some of the estates and were built in such a position as to gain the maximum amount of wind power; they worked faster than the old mills. Clay Ghaut and Montpelier mills were built at the same time, in 1785. John Pinney did not convert his estate to wind-power for grinding cane until 1790. Coconut Walk mill is dated 1805 and Golden Rock 1811. Twelve cattle mills still worked until the end of the nineteenth century. The round stone towers of the windmills, of which one can still see the remains in many parts of the island, were 30 to 40 feet high and measured 20 feet in diameter at floor level, tapering off to 15 feet at the top. The walls were three feet thick. Coconut Walk mill was the highest because it was built at a low altitude. These sugar mills were of the tower type in which a rotatable cap supports the sails on top of a fixed body (built of stone in the case of Nevis). Originally the cogs were made of wood which was silent when running, and they were remarkably durable. Subsequently the cogs were made of iron.

The process of sugar making involved firstly cutting the cane in the fields using machetes or cutlasses to cut the stalk, tying the cane in bundles and loading these onto donkeys or horses for transport to the mill. Upon arrival there the cane was crushed between iron rollers; metal-lined wooden troughs underneath collected the juice which was conveyed to the boiler house down a long wooden spout. It was then clarified by heating it with a small quantity of lime which broke down the glucose, enabling the juice to crystallize. The clear juice was ladled into successive coppers, each smaller than the last, heated by hot gases passing underneath. It was boiled down into a thick syrup which ran off

The steam mill and sugar factory of the New River Estate were the last to process sugar on Nevis in 1956 into a large shallow wooden box to cool before being potted into hogsheads (barrels with holes in the bottom). Muscovado sugar was left in the hogsheads and the substance which dripped out was the molasses. Rum was made from the skimmings of the first boiling of the cane juice which was used to ferment equal quantities of molasses. Lime for the processing of sugar was produced from the coral found on the beaches; there were several lime kilns situated on the windward side of the island. The kiln below Coconut Walk is still in use today; the lime it produces is used for building purposes.

The first sugar plantations were established here in the second half of the seventeenth century. They were not large, the average size being about 100 acres; some were smaller and only one or two were over 200 acres. Before the end of the century the plantations were well established and Nevis was recognised as an important sugar island. This was in spite of the natural disasters which affected the whole economy, such as the earthquake in 1680 when the main town, Jamestown, was engulfed by a tidal wave and when an outbreak of smallpox and malignant fevers caused countless deaths. The greatest setback to prosperity was in 1706 when the French invaded and plundered the island and took with them 3000 slaves, half of the labour force. A hurricane the following year added to the catastrophe. £75 000 was paid in compensation by the colonial power for the 'ravages of war' and £674 was contributed from friends in Boston for the relief of distress. From that time onwards, the planters on Nevis acquired the reputation of being stubborn and difficult to negotiate with and, for at least the next fifty years, pleaded their inability to pay full taxes. Contemporary descriptions of Nevis emphasise the decline that had set in and how the number of inhabitants had decreased. Sugar production took several decades to recover; the remaining inhabitants worked hard and improved their methods of farming, while the best of the planters manured the cane and used the ashes from the boiler houses as fertilizer.

Until the end of the eighteenth century the sugar industry on Nevis continued to expand and the total population grew from 7000 in 1678 to over 11 000 in 1774. Incredible though it may seem, at that time Nevis was a more important commercial entity than New York!

The decline of sugar had started long before the emancipation of the slaves in 1834. The poor soil and the stones on Nevis had always been a physical constraint to the amount of sugar that could be grown compared to St Kitts, which has a rich, volcanic soil. After a hundred years of monoculture the yields of sugar began to decrease year by year and the cost of running a sugar estate had doubled within a century. In 1763 the price of sugar fell from 38s 6d to 35s per cwt and there was competition from Cuba and the French islands whose sugar sold in the European markets at a far lower price than English sugar could be sold. After the American War of Independence Nevis lost her sugar markets on the American mainland as well as losing essential imports from there. In 1784 the Nevis legislature claimed the island would shortly be forced out of sugar production by a combination of falling prices and rising costs. There had been severe hurricanes in 1780 and 1781 followed by a drought which caused the failure of an entire sugar crop.

Following emancipation many of the estates on Nevis were so heavily in debt that most of the sum of £145 967 paid in compensation to the owners went to creditors and mortgages. Debts were foreclosed on and credit became hard to come by. Although there were few alternatives for the freed slaves there was little enthusiasm for working on the land and farming became unpopular. Estates changed hands and land sold for between £4 and £10 per acre. Another severe blow to sugar production was when the *Navigation* laws were repealed in 1849. These laws had protected the planters and when the preferential duty on sugar was finally withdrawn in 1852 the price fell by almost 20% and wages were halved. A description of life in 1871 was given by John Alexander Burk Isles who was the Colonial Secretary at the time. The population was then estimated at 12 000 and during the previous year 5000 hogsheads of sugar (a hogshead is approximately 1800 pounds weight), 2000 puncheons of molasses and 5000 puncheons of sugar had been produced. There were then twenty steam-powered factories. The windmills were going out of use for various reasons: the new steam mills extracted 15% more juice, there was a lack of labour to manage the sails and also a shortage of hardwood to repair and maintain the working parts of the windmills. Windmills were also far slower to crush the cane than the steam engines.

The modernisation of the sugar factories and the new capital brought in by men such as the Honourable Graham Briggs, who owned five large and nine smaller estates here by the 1870s, did little to halt the decline of sugar. In Europe sugar beet was becoming established as a profitable crop, and sugar from the West Indies was consequently losing favour. Muscovado sugar was produced in Nevis until after the 1939-1945 war, but its small factories were uneconomic to operate and were gradually forced to shut down. Machinery from disused mills was bought by sugar producers in the French islands of Martinique and Guadeloupe. In 1912 a sugar processing factory was built on St Kitts; much of

the cane grown on the island was then shipped from Newcastle to Basseterre, which added to the producers' costs.

There were six windmills operating in 1900: Dunbars, Zetland, Hanley, Montpelier, Powells and Clay Ghaut (whose sails turned for the very last time in 1940). Ten steam engines were in operation at Prospect, Hamilton's (which was the largest) Cane Garden, Old Manor, Hard Times Estate, Fothergills, New River, Maddens Farm, and Round Hill. The last one to operate was New River in 1956. It was then Government-owned, having been bought from the Maynard family. By 1920 half of the sixty-eight estates were owned by non-residents. Gillespie Bros, a firm of English financiers, had bought up many estates including those which had belonged to the Hon. Graham Briggs. Profits had become so small that owners were forced to sell. It is not easy to find sugar cane growing on Nevis today – only a few acres of cane are grown, perhaps for fodder – but it is still possible to see evidence of the past, when Nevis was called a sugar island.

The remains of a sugar mill at Montpelier, now part of a hotel. The mill was built around 1785 and was still in use in 1900

⑤ Churches, chapels and tombstones

The five Anglican churches of St Paul, St Thomas, St James, St George and St John were all built in the seventeenth century to serve the needs of the English settlers. The first buildings would have been wooden; since then each church has been rebuilt in local stone on or near the original foundations. The plaques in the churches and the tombstones both inside and outside in the graveyard reveal a wealth of historical information and are well worth a study.

St Paul's is the parish church of Charlestown and was rebuilt in the 1890s. On either side of the altar there are stained glass windows to the memory of the Revd Daniel Gatward Davies who was Rector of the parishes of St Paul's and St Thomas from 1812 to 1825. He subsequently became the first Bishop of Antigua. He and the Revd John Pemberton of St George's church were the first Anglican priests to initiate a programme of conversions amongst the negro population before the emancipation of the slaves. The annual salary of each clergyman was 16 000 pounds of sugar. It was paid irregularly and its cash value depended on the quality of the sugar as well as the price it was sold for after duties and the shipping costs had been paid. Little wonder the clergy had a reputation for being indolent and frequently absent, caring little for their parishioners or for the unconverted slaves.

St Thomas's church on the leeward side of the island was the first church to be built on Nevis, in 1643. It contains plaques and tombstones of people such as Jacob Lake, who was one of the earliest Governors of Nevis and various members of the Huggins family. Outside are the graves of members of the Khuri Singh family, who were one of the very few Indian families to settle on the island.

Cottle church has recently been restored. A tranquil and solitary church, it was originally built by Thomas John Cottle, who owned Round Hill Estate and who was for several years president of the Nevis Assembly. He wanted to provide a church where his family and slaves might worship together. The church was opened on 5 May 1824 when a solemn service was held by the Rector of St Paul's, in place of a consecration. (None of the churches on Nevis had yet been consecrated by a Bishop, as the island was not visited by one until 1824.) In 1861 Sir Graham Briggs, who had bought Round Hill Estate, repaired the church which became known as St Marks-at-Ease. By the end of the century however, the church had again fallen into a state of ruin.

St James Windward is close to the Atlantic. First built in 1679, it now contains a crucifix with a black Christ. There are only three others like it in the Caribbean. St George's church in Gingerland has several interesting tombstones: the Revd Pemberton is buried here (1870), having been born on Nevis and been Rector of St George's and St John's for sixty years. The Revd John Jones, who was Rector from 1890 to 1898, buried four of his children during that time. Originally built in 1670, the date above the lintel of the west door indicates the year the church was extended and repaired. An earthquake in 1950 badly damaged the sanctuary which had to be rebuilt in the northern transept. St John's Fig Tree, so called because of its original proximity to a fig tree, was Lady Nelson's parish. Inside there is a monument to her parents – the Woodwards. The date 1838 engraved over the door is the date the present building was completed, although two side aisles were added in 1890. The roof ridges were altered early in the twentieth century and in 1961 the wooden floor was replaced by a concrete one.

There are seven Methodist chapels; the main one is in Charlestown. Others are at Gingerland, New River, Combermere, Fountain and Clifton. The first to be built in Charlestown was dedicated to Dr Thomas Coke in 1790. He brought Methodism to the West Indies at the end of the eighteenth century. The Methodists were the first missionaries to work in Nevis for the conversion of non-believers to Christianity, and their work was opposed by some of the plantocracy who suspected a Methodist connection with Wilberforce's campaign for the abolition of slavery. In 1797 an attempt to burn down the first chapel was made by planters who objected to the preaching of Revd John Brownell against the immorality of the island as well as the gambling and cock fighting on Sundays. The damage to the chapel was not beyond repair, but a new and bigger chapel was built near to the foundations of the old one. It was designed and built under the supervision of Revd Jesse Pilcher who was a missionary and master builder on Nevis from 1824 to 1846. Funds to pay for the chapel were raised locally; there was also a grant made by the Nevis House of Assembly. In 1793 there were already 400 members of the Methodist Church here and by 1826 records show there were 802, of whom 601 were slaves. Behind the Methodist manse are several tombstones of missionaries and their families who died here. The tombstone of the Revd Thomas Stonemand states that he travelled from Nova Scotia, but was actually 'dead on arrival'. The Revd Bell died at the early age of twenty-six. Nevis owes a great deal to the Methodist church, to its spiritual work as well as the schooling it provided before education became a responsibility of the colonial power.

The Roman Catholic chapel of St Theresa's in Charlestown and the chapel at Taylor's Pasture (Gingerland) were both built after 1945. A third chapel has been built recently on Westbury Road. When Nevis was first colonised Roman Catholics were actively discouraged from settling there. A law was passed to this effect by the Leeward Island Legislature in 1701; the same Council discussed the subject of Catholic emancipation in 1795 but this time it was the British Parliament who could not agree to Catholics being given the right to vote and stand for election to the Council or Assembly. When St Kitts and Nevis became a single colony in 1882 Roman Catholics were fully accepted on the islands and a priest travelled from St Kitts to take services in private houses until the chapels were built. It was in accordance with Columbus' practice to name the surrounding islands after the shrines of Mary: Guadeloupe, Montserrat, Redonda, Antigua. These islands form the shape of a crown. The shrine after which this island is named, 'Sancta Maria de las Nieves', is venerated in the basilica of Mary Major in Rome. This is an alternative theory for why the island became known as Nevis. In 1968 the feast of 'Sancta Maria de las Nieves' was officially celebrated. The priest had brought from Rome a good copy of the shrine and installed it in the church in Charlestown; there was a small copy in Gingerland. The feast on 5 August is observed on the nearest Sunday. The chapels are modern and simple with the pictures of the Stations of the Cross painted by American artists Dorothy Cleary and Betty Winebrenner.

The remains of a Jewish cemetery are located in Government Road, Charlestown. Over twenty tombstones have been found, dated between 1679 and 1730. One stone has two hands inscribed upon it indicating that the grave was that of a Rabbi. Another close to a tree reveals an hourglass and a branch, probably the grave of a female who died young. Jewish merchants came here in the mid-seventeenth century having been expelled from Brazil by the Portuguese. A census of the island taken in 1701 listed five Jewish families and fourteen people. Recent archaeological research has been undertaken to locate the site of the synagogue which was referred to by the Rector of St Paul's in 1724. The Jewish community contributed much to the life and history of Nevis.

Many new sects of Christianity built churches and chapels here in the twentieth century, particularly after 1945: Evangelical churches such as the Church of God of Mount Carmel, the Church of God Prophecy, the Emmas Chapel, the Jehovah's Witnesses, the Wesleyan Holiness and the Pentecostal Mission. Seventh Day Adventists started here as early as 1904. These churches are funded and partly organised by parent churches in the USA. Travelling round the island on Sundays one sees many people on their way to and from church, on foot, by car or in church minibuses, women and children in their best and prettiest clothes, men in their suits. The windows and doors of the churches and chapels are always wide open so the hymn singing can be heard and enjoyed by passers by.

Religion still plays an important part in the lives of Nevisians, so that Sunday is a day for church as well as a day of rest.

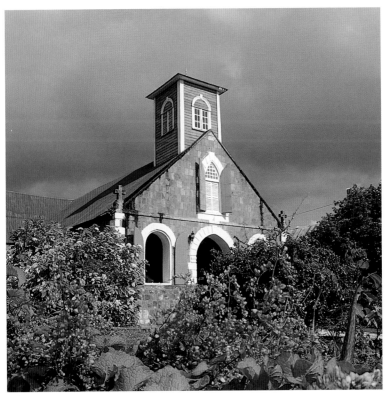

▲ St Paul's church, Charlestown

⑥ Government House

Guarded by a smartly uniformed policeman and commanding panoramic views of St Kitts and beyond stands an imposing house, the residence of the Queen's representative for Nevis. The house was built in 1909 using local stone; the design is West Indian 'colonial' with Victorian architectural influences. During colonial times Government House was the official residence for the visiting Governors of the Leeward Isles. After the union with St Kitts the administrator for Nevis, who was called the Honourable Warden, resided at Government House. When statehood was attained in 1967 the Permanent Secretary for Nevis' affairs was entitled to live in the official residence. After Independence and the re-establishment of the Nevis Island Assembly a higher level of Government representation was felt necessary, hence the Deputy Governor-General of St Kitts-Nevis now resides there. When in 1966 Queen Elizabeth II and Prince Philip paid a state visit to Nevis they were welcomed at Government House by several hundred school children as well as official guests. Again in 1985 the Royal couple visited Government House. It is used for official receptions and functions and any visiting official or important guest to the island is requested to sign the guest book. At Christmas time an annual party is given by the Deputy Governor for the handicapped people of the community. The Nevis and Federal flags are flown when the incumbent is in residence.

◀ Guard at Government House

▼ Government House, Charlestown, was built in 1909

⑦ Fort Charles and the defence of Nevis

'The chief fortress of the island – called Charles Fort – stands on the south-west point of the Island. The road for the shipping is under the cannon of this fort and the town (called Charlestown) is in the bottom of this bay entirely easterly of it. The shipping rides safest here of any open road on the four islands ... Charles Fort was laid out on a larger plan than the forts usually were on these islands ... I imagine the whole circumference to contain 6 acres. To landward on two sides tis an old ruinous rampart and ditch, the other two sides are to seaward and are well faced with stone, the platforms are paved and a low rampart wall but no merlons ... the cannons are well mounted ...'

This description was written in 1734 by a military gentleman reporting to the Lords of the Trades and Plantations concerning the defences in the West Indies. At that time there were thirteen guns positioned on Fort Charles ranging from 36 to 6 pounders. In addition around the island were twelve open batteries in strategic positions ... *'small forts, something like platt bastions, faced with mason's work and merlons on the parapets, cannons too are mounted on them ...'* All that remains of Fort Charles is the perimeter wall, the old cistern or well and the powder magazine where gunpowder, muskets, balls and guns were stored. The above report also recommended that *'Saddle Hill (that is inaccessible by nature), should be fortified and made into a safe retreat for the inhabitants and their effects'*. The building commenced in 1740. Planters were ordered to send their slaves with tools to construct a series of walls extending to a length of 1600 feet which were at different heights on the seaward side with a watchtower on the highest peak. On the inward side there was a rampart the entire length of the hillside. Thanks to the stalwart work of local volunteers, parts of this battery are now visible.

Fort Ashby, which was built to defend Jamestown, is a mere relic and the Redoubt at Newcastle has been demolished to make room for an extension to the airport. On Hurricane Hill, overlooking Oalie Bay, Ian and Freda Holland, who own the property, initiated and have completed the restoration of Fort Codrington. It commands a strategic position overlooking the Narrows. Christopher Codrington was Governor of the Leeward Isles around the turn of the seventeenth century (he also owned plantations in Barbados). It was he who maintained that: 'All turns on the mastery of the sea, if we have it, our islands are safe; if the French have it, we cannot raise enough men in all the islands to hold one of them.'

There were two occasions when the French invaded Nevis. A landing in 1706 under d'Iberville was a successful attempt to plunder the island rather than to capture it. The militia were soon overcome and surrendered to the enemy at Morning Star. The slaves however put up a braver resistance and it was said they were pursued far up the mountainside. Over half a million pounds' worth of damage was done to property; homes and buildings were ruined and pilfered, crops were destroyed and half of the entire slave population was captured and taken off the island. (The owner of Zetland Plantation set fire to his house rather than let the French destroy it.) The enemy had embarked their troops at Green Bay, south of Low Point on the south-west coast, which is mainly inaccessible.

Following this humiliation, Acts were passed by the Assembly to repair the fortifications (1706) and for regulating and disciplining the militia (1721). The defence depended mainly on the militia, men between the ages of fourteen and sixty, and those refusing to serve, such as the few Quakers who lived here until 1709, were subject to penalties. The colonial power was disinclined to spend much money on defence though a small company of infantry soldiers was stationed here from the Royal Scots, and later from the King's Own Scottish Borderers.

Fort Charles was the scene of an historic meeting of the Nevis Council under their President John Herbert in February 1782. Brimstone Hill on St Kitts had been under siege from the French. Admiral Hood, having cleverly outmanoeuvred Admiral de Grasse and the French navy before Basseterre, had moved away. The ruling planters knew that any attempt to resist the French fleet of twenty-four sail of line as well as other small craft would be useless, so they negotiated their own terms of capitulation. This was the only time that Nevis was occupied by a foreign power; the occupation lasted less than a year and no one seemed to have borne malice against the occupiers. The French commanders were polite to the planters whose only fear was that the indiscretions of the negroes would offend the French. During the occupation food ran short until supplies were brought in by ships flying a flag of a neutral country. Nevis was restored to the British under the *Treaty of Versailles* in 1783, as was St Kitts. The fear of impending invasion was removed from the Caribbean waters after the battle of Trafalgar and the *Treaty of Paris* in 1814. Defending the island ceased to be important, so Fort Charles and the other small forts fell into disuse.

The first Naval victory of the United States took place off Nevis near Indian Castle in 1799. A 38-gun frigate, USS *Constellation*, was in confrontation with a 40-gun French frigate, *L'Insurage*. The two ships exchanged fire for over an hour until the heavier guns of the American frigate caused serious damage to the *L'Insurage* which was forced to strike its colours. Only two Americans out of a crew of 419 were lost. Forty-two Frenchmen perished. A picture of this battle has been presented to the Nevis Historical and Conservation Society.

▲ The old well at Fort Charles

⑧ The Nelson connection

Horatio Nelson's association with Nevis began in 1785 following his appointment the previous year to command HMS *Boreas*, based at English Harbour in Antigua. He was there to enforce the *Navigation Acts*, which were being violently flouted following the *Treaty of Versailles* in 1783 which had recognised the independence of the thirteen American colonies. The end of the hostilities against the French brought little relief for the inhabitants of Nevis. The merchants from New England who had previously traded here were now foreigners and as such were forbidden to trade with British colonies, but an agreeable arrangement continued so that American goods such as timber, various provisions, horses and hides could be imported into Nevis and the other colonial islands in exchange for sugar. Nelson was not prepared to compromise – he could not ignore the evidence he saw of American vessels trading with the planters and he regarded the latter as vagabonds and as rebellious as the Americans.

Visiting Nevis in the course of his duties Nelson found four American vessels heavily laden with cargo and flying an island flag (white with a red cross). They were ordered to hoist their true flag and to depart within twenty-four hours. The Americans refused to do this. Nelson therefore questioned some of the crew in his own cabin. The crew members confessed to being American. This raised much opposition and fury from the planters and officials and even the Governor was against his interference as Nelson had also impounded the goods on the ships. The merchants of Nevis made a claim for £40 000 against Nelson for this action. A lawyer was engaged for the defence who suggested a story that the crew members had given their evidence to Nelson under bodily fear as the sentry at the cabin door was a man with a drawn sword. The Marshall tried to arrest Nelson, but the Captain hid himself and actually remained on board for eight weeks to avoid being sent to the local gaol. Mr John Herbert was at this time President of Nevis. He showed great generosity to Nelson and offered to put up £10 000 bail for him. This was in spite of the fact that he was also affected by Nelson's strict policy. The prosecuting lawyer won the case despite the pleadings of the defence that ships of war were not justified in searching American vessels and that it should be the task of the customs officials and the Governor of the island. Nelson pleaded his case so well (his expenses were eventually paid for by the Crown) that the goods carried by the boats were condemned.

▲ The Nelson plaque on the old gatepost of Montpelier House

Nelson used the freshwater well near the lagoon at Cotton Ground to provide drinking water for HMS *Boreas*; kegs were rowed ashore to be filled up. It was said that he climbed up to the battery on Saddle Hill to search the horizon for offending vessels. He was unpopular and unwelcomed by society here until Prince William, as Captain of HMS *Pegasus*, was also appointed to be based at English Harbour. He and Nelson were then constantly in each other's company on official and social occasions.

Mr John Herbert, who had helped Nelson in connection with the lawsuit, lived at Montpelier, then the largest house on the island. His niece Fanny Nisbet lived with him. She had been born on Nevis twenty-two years before when her father William Woodward had been a judge on the island. He had died of a fatal illness and during his last days had been cared for by a Dr Josiah Nisbet. Fanny married the doctor, who within a few months of their wedding became ill. Their son Josiah was born in England and her husband died there in 1781. Her uncle, who was himself a widower, invited his orphaned and widowed niece to share his home and she took over the supervision of the household. Her first meeting with Nelson was at a dinner party at Montpelier House, although Nelson had already met her five-year old son on an informal visit to Montpelier. It is doubtful whether either of them fell passionately or instantly in love with the other. Nelson had already been enamoured by two other women and Fanny's chances of remarriage at that age and with a small son were slight. Perhaps it was mutual loneliness that was the incentive to their betrothal. Fanny, who knew of Nelson's reputation as an aloof and strict disciplinarian with regard to his work, was soon to find an affectionate and warm side to his nature. Her uncle, who by now had a great respect for Nelson, had promised to help him financially. A Captain's salary in those days would certainly not stretch to keeping a wife and a child in the manner to which Fanny had been accustomed. The marriage took place at Montpelier House on 11 March 1787. Marriages rarely took place in a church and it was the Rector of St John's who recorded the marriage in his register. The society of the day gathered together in the opulent mansion for the wedding. A special dinner service of Royal Worcester plate was cast in England for the occasion. Prince William gave away the bride, who was dressed in lace. Nelson and the Prince were in full dress uniforms of blue, white and gold. Nelson wrote to a friend subsequently to say that 'indeed before I married her I never knew happiness and I am morally certain that she will continue to make me happy for the rest of my days'. Alas this was not to be. In March of the same year Nelson sailed for England in the *Boreas* followed by his wife and stepson. John Herbert also left Nevis soon afterwards and with his great wealth settled in Cavendish Square in London. (The Prince was also recalled to London in disgrace after a bout of extravagant debauchery amongst the ladies of Quebec!) For five years the Nelsons lived in Norfolk at Burnham Thorpe at the parsonage house of his father. It was not until England was brought into another major war in Europe against the French that Nelson was again given command of a ship, HMS *Agamemnon*, in which he sailed to the Mediterranean in 1793.

In the naval operations which took place before the Battle of Trafalgar, Nelson once more sailed in Caribbean waters. He was pursuing the Admiral of the French Fleet, Admiral Villeneuve. He arrived at Barbados in early June 1805, then went to Antigua to water his ships, passing Nevis on his way back across the Atlantic. One wonders what his feelings were as he saw the cloud-covered mountain and reflected upon his marriage which had been one of dull domesticity compared to the passionate feelings he now had for Lady Hamilton. Nelson died from wounds sustained at the Battle of Trafalgar in 1805, knowing that the battle was being won thanks to his tactics and the superiority of the British gunnery. His last thoughts were for Lady Hamilton and their daughter Horatia. England had lost one of its greatest heroes and the memory of him remains immortal.

Fanny was given a state pension of £2000 a year for life to add to the £1000 a year she received from Nelson's estate. She had been abandoned by Nelson several years before the Battle of Trafalgar: her last efforts to be reconciled to him had been rejected. She remained loyal to the memory of her husband until she died in 1831. She spent her last years living at Exmouth in Devonshire and lies buried in the nearby church at Littleham. The Revd William Nelson inherited his brother's title and he received a pension of £5000 a year as well as £1000 to purchase a family estate. The viscountcy is still in existence.

⑨ The museums of Nevis

The Museum of Nevis History (at the birthplace of Alexander Hamilton) was built in time for the opening to take place on Independence Day, 19 September 1982. It was opened by ex-Congressman Bertram Baker who was born on Nevis. Finance for the building came from US Aid and from donations to the Nevis Historical and Conservation Society; the Government of St Kitts-Nevis provided money for labour and contingencies. The upper floor, badly damaged in Hurricane Hugo, is used for meetings of the Nevis Assembly; visitors can see the mace lying on the meeting table.

There is a substantial amount of material on display relating to Alexander Hamilton who was born on Nevis on 11 January 1757. His maternal grandfather, Dr Fawcett, had a small estate in Gingerland as well as practising medicine. His mother had inherited a house on the foreshore in Charlestown where she went to live with James Hamilton and where she gave birth to Alexander. When Alexander was nine years of age the family left Nevis and moved to St Croix where his mother died soon afterwards. James Hamilton was related to the famed Hamilton family of both St Kitts and Nevis, but alas he seemed unable to make a success of any venture. Alexander left St Croix at the age of sixteen and with the help of friends went to study in New York State. He became the First Secretary of the American Treasury but not before he had fought against the English in the War of American Independence at Yorktown and elsewhere, and had become a successful lawyer. He was the first to advocate the federation of the American states which was eventually adopted. No wonder that Americans who come to Nevis are

▲ The Alexander Hamilton plaque at the Museum of Nevis History, Charlestown

inspired with feelings of respect for his birthplace and that a museum has been built on the foundations.

The display of artefacts found on Nevis dates from the pre-Columbian period to the eighteenth century and includes pottery and ornaments excavated in 1986 near Hickmans, which has been dated AD500.

The discovery of these and other Amerindian artefacts has confirmed that the island was inhabited prior to European settlement in 1628, probably as early as 2000BC. The Arawaks preceded the Caribs; both were from the same ethnic group but had different characteristics and had migrated from different parts of South America. They were subsistence farmers growing manioc (cassava) maize and sweet potatoes, fruits and vegetables. They smoked tobacco, which they called 'cohiba'. They were fishermen, carving their boats from tree trunks using tools made from conch shells. They ate iguanas and turtles, and their main stew pot, the 'pepper pot' made from clay, is still copied and used today. The Caribs were more aggressive than the Arawaks, indeed Columbus regarded them as cannibals. 'Oualie' is the name which it is thought the Caribs gave to Nevis. Thomas Warner made peaceful terms with the Carib Chief Tegremond when he first arrived on St Kitts in 1623. It was the Caribs who taught the English to make 'mawby', a local drink cheaper than imported wine, and introduced them to manioc, sweet potatoes and yams. The Carib raids were a constant threat to the early colonists and a continued menace to navigators until the seventeenth century. The Caribs who survived settled on Grenada, St Vincent, St Lucia and Dominica where a community of them still exists today.

The history of Nevis, its architecture, its churches and schools, its customs, its agriculture past and present and its ecology are all well illustrated in the various displays. A complete set of drawings of the Redoubt are on view.

The Nelson Museum, situated close to the Bath Hotel, contains a collection of memorabilia much of which belonged to the late Mr Robert Adams and his wife. It was originally housed at his residence at Morning Star where it was visited by various members of the British Royal family. It is a unique collection of letters, pictures, objects d'art, including china plates used at the Nelson-Nisbet wedding.

Amongst the copies of historical documents in the Nelson Museum is the account of the infamous case 'The King vs Edward Huggins Senior Esq.', brought by the authorities who felt 'they were bound in humanity and from regard to the credit of the colony publicly to reprobate and make it a subject for legal investigation'. The charge against Edward Huggins was cruelty to his slaves, who were punished by his son Peter because they had attempted to run away rather than obey his orders to carry dung or throw grass into the cattle pens at midnight, which was contrary to the *Melioration Act* of 1797. To make an example of them, Huggins had a number of slaves taken to the market place on 23 January 1810 where almost thirty of them were flogged unmercifully. The floggings took place within sight and hearing of various people including some of the magistrates who, by their inaction, were in fact condoning an act which they knew was illegal. Two hundred and thirty-six lashes were inflicted on one slave and one of the female slaves died following the flogging. Five months later the trial took place and the facts were not disputed by Huggins. His defending council argued to the jury against Huggins' obligation to respect the *Melioration Act* of 1797, speaking of it in a most contemptuous way. The defence was effectual and Huggins was acquitted. The whole episode was an outrage against humanity and decency; much publicity was given to the case (and a later one against Huggins) and the information used to great advantage to further the cause for the emancipation of the slaves. Mr Huggins was a successful planter at a time when many other planters were beginning to go under, and the case revealed that a master prosecuted for the abuse of his slaves was sure to have plenty of supporters, well aware the case could easily have been their own. In a letter sent by the Earl of Liverpool, who was Secretary of State, to Governor Elliot of the Leeward Isles he wrote: 'I am commanded by HRH the Prince Regent to direct you to remove from that honourable situation any magistrate who actually witnessed the infliction of punishment without interference ... this to be done with a degree of publicity to illustrate HRH's reprobation of such a culpable remission on their part ...'

There are also exhibits of pre-Columbian Nevis, the history of slavery, sugar processing and pictures by Eva Wilkins, a famous artist on Nevis. There is space allocated for displays with different themes of educational value. The Archives are housed here, which include church records and source material on the geology of the area, history, architecture, genealogy and other subjects. There are book shops in both museums and the proceeds go to the funding of the Nevis Historical and Conservation Society.

The Society plays a vital role on the island. Not only does it publicise the historical aspects of the island and the importance of preservation, but it has also initiated an awareness of environmental matters influencing education in the school system. The Field Studies Programme is also organised by the Society. Several teams of archaeologists have carried out projects in recent years, including excavations at the Jewish Cemetery, Coconut Walk, the Upper Round Road and a slave village at Montravers. The University of Southampton in the United Kingdom has a team who come annually to study the fortifications of the island, prehistoric settlements and early pottery, etc.

At Fothergills Heritage Village the Tourist Board have built examples of houses which were lived in by the earliest settlers on Nevis, from the Arawaks, the slaves and Nevisians, through post-emancipation until the late twentieth century. It is a good exhibition showing how the earliest homes were constructed, the materials used and how they were set on corners of large stones so that moving to an alternative site was possible, and frequently took place.

▲ A replica of an early Nevisian house at Fothergills Heritage Village

The Nevis Historical and Conservation Society and the Island Administration have received a grant of US$700,000 from the Caribbean Regional Conservation Program and the EU to develop the Bath Estate, stream and bogs. The goal is to form a major regional example of how an environmentally threatened area can, when properly managed, become an economic asset to the island.

⑩ The Bath Hotel and others

Built by John Huggins in 1778 for the cost of £40 000, the Bath House hotel accommodated fifty guests and made use of the sulphurous hot water springs close by to provide medicinal baths for those who desired them. Water from these springs had long been recognised as beneficial for various ailments including rheumatism and gout. As early as 1716 the Revd Smith related how often he bathed in the stream to the great benefit of his health. The hotel was well built and spacious, 200 ft long and 100 ft broad, several storeys high, and included a ballroom and a large dining hall. Its gardens were compared to the hanging gardens of Babylon with roses, ferneries and stucco statuary as well as goldfish ponds, stables and wine cellars. Bathing took place in a two-storey, substantially built bath-house. The toilet rooms were above, and below was the hot bath, about 30 feet square, filled with crystal clear, soft, smooth water. Nevis became

▲ The ruins of the old Bath Hotel

famous for this hotel; pleasure seekers young and old from the fashionable world of the West Indies as well as from Europe came to enjoy the hotel and the attractions of the whole island. Henry Nelson Coleridge during his visit to Nevis in 1825 commented that the building was too large but that 'an invalid with a good servant might take up his quarters here with more comfort than in any other house of public reception in the West Indies ...'. He describes three plunge baths on terraces one above the other with the temperature of the water varying between 50 and 100°F. The lowest and largest bath was used as a turtle crawl, where the poor creatures flounced about until overcome by sulphur fumes when they were removed and subsequently made into soup.

In 1870 the hotel and baths were closed. Mr Paton in his booklet, *Down the Islands*, written in 1890, gave a sad description of the hotel: the gardens were being neglected, the hotel was a massive ruin, the roof having fallen in, and ferns and mosses were growing out of the masonry and crevices; the verandahs had fallen away and the windows and casements had been used as firewood. It was a picture of desolation and decay; no longer did the rich come, there was no more laughter, music, pomp and splendour, no matchmaking, dancing or flirting.

Before the 1914–18 war the hotel was bought and restored by Messrs Gillespie Bros and Co; two galleries were added to the

hotel and one of the baths was rebuilt for use as a health resort. A limited number of visitors were accommodated at ten shillings each per day. During the Great War it was used for the training of the West Indian Regiment. By 1920 the dining room was in use again and on Friday nights visitors used to be brought from St Kitts and off cruise ships to dine there for the price of two shillings and sixpence. It was a popular meeting place for local residents who, if unable to visit the baths for therapeutic treatment, could buy a bottle of the healing water for use at home. The building received considerable damage in the 1950 earthquake. In 1970 an attempt was made to restore the hotel by a new owner Norman Fowler who inherited a large fortune from his lover who had died under suspicious circumstances in his bath at their London home. In 1971 Normal Fowler died aged 44. The death certificate simply stated: "Coroner's inquest subsequently held death by drowning in hot water bath at Bath Hotel."

There are now many hotels around the island, some close to the shore, others on the hillsides. Nisbet Plantation Beach Club, Old Manor Hotel, Monpelier, Hermitage and Golden Rock are based on old plantation homes. Others such as Mount Nevis, Oalie Beach Hotel, the Inn at Cades Bay have all been built recently. The largest hotel is the Four Seasons Hotel situated alongside Pinneys Beach with its own adjoining 18-hole golf course. Once again Nevis is famous for its hotels, attracting tourists from many parts of the world.

The Four Seasons Hotel on Pinneys Beach

⑪ Beaches

The beaches on Nevis are some of the best in the Caribbean. Pinneys beach stretches along four miles with golden sand fringed with coconut palms. Mount Nevis rises in the background and St Kitts is seen across the water. Bathing is safe and the sea warm all the year round. Cades Bay stretches from Cliffdwellers to Hurricane Hill and includes the Oualie Beach Club and hotel where there is a variety of water sports available including scuba diving, snorkelling and wind surfing. On the north side of

Newcastle Beach at Nisbet

▲ Pinney's Beach

Hurricane Hill is a narrow lane leading to an isolated and long stretch of sand, without shade and with no facilities, sometimes known as Lovers' Beach. The beach in front of the Nisbet Plantation Hotel is also most attractive, palm fringed and facing the reef and the southernmost tip of St Kitts. Herbert's Beach is west of the Nisbet Plantation and has some good snorkelling with clear water.

The coastline on the windward side of the island is mainly stony and rocky apart from two small bays used by fishermen. The sea is wild with strong surf and powerful undercurrents, making it too dangerous for swimming. At Indian Castle there is a long stretch of nearly white sand; it is a place for walking unless one is a strong swimmer as the sea is invariably rough with strong undertows. To reach this beach turn right in Gingerland down Hanleys Road, then left passing the race course until the beach can be seen. The southern shores of Nevis are rocky – no beaches, no road or easy access; the French in 1706 chose this inhospitable stretch of coast to land and invade the island.

⑫ Walks

1 Nevis Peak There are at least two routes which lead to the summit of Mount Nevis (3232 feet). The most popular one starts from Dunbar Hill above Zetlands Plantation. It is strongly recommended to ask for a guide as after the first few miles of the walk the path is not easy to find and the final part of the ascent is in fact a scramble.

2 The Source This walk towards the source of the island's water supply takes about two to three hours. The trees and ferns to be seen on this walk provide interest as well as shade for a large part of the way. Start at Rawlins reservoir where the path is easily found, bearing northwards with fine views

Nevis Peak from Gingerland

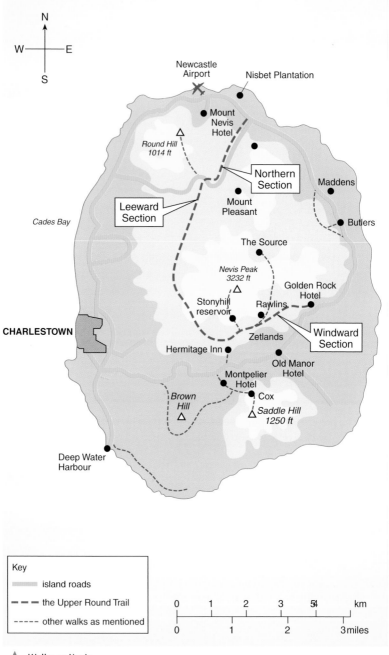

N

W —●— E

S

Newcastle
Airport ✈

Nisbet Plantation ●

● Mount
Nevis
Hotel

△ *Round Hill
1014 ft*

●

Northern
Section

Leeward
Section

● Maddens

Mount
Pleasant ●

● Butlers

Cades Bay

The Source ●

*Nevis Peak
3232 ft*
△

Golden Rock
Hotel ●

Stonyhill
reservoir ● Rawlins ● ●

CHARLESTOWN

Zetlands

Windward
Section

Hermitage Inn ●

Old Manor
Hotel ●

Montpelier
Hotel ●
● Cox

*Brown
Hill*
△

△ *Saddle Hill
1250 ft*

● Deep Water
Harbour

Key

▓▓▓ island roads

— — the Upper Round Trail

----- other walks as mentioned

0	1	2	3	5 4	km
0		1		2	3 miles

▲ Walks on Nevis

▲ Newcastle Beach at Nisbet

overlooking Golden Rock Estate and the sea before winding upwards into the forest. To protect the island's water supply it is recommended that you turn back here. Further along, a somewhat ancient ladder mounts the collecting chamber of the reservoir. Under no circumstances attempt to climb the ladder, it is very dangerous.

3 Butlers to Maddens At the top of Butlers village a road to the right leads all the way to Maddens farm. This is not a long walk but the views of the sea from here are superb, as are those of the mountain (known as Butler's Mountain or Back Hill).

4 The Upper Round Road The Upper Round Road Trail is approximately nine miles in total connecting Golden Rock Estate on the windward side of the island with Nisbet Plantation in the north. The path is the original Upper Round Road which was used to connect several of the sugar estates and which is still used by people who work small plots and gardens in the vicinity. It can be approached from various points, from Golden Rock Hotel, from above Zetlands or Hermitage Inn or taking Government Road in Charlestown and continuing uphill passing the old buildings at Hamilton Estate until the concrete road ends and the path is visible.

5 Long Point and Dogwood Estate This walk along the coast is now also a bike trail and extends along the coast from Bath village to the Dogwood Estate. There are stunning views of the mountain and of Saddle Hill from the shore and the vegetation consists mainly of acacia bush and brightly coloured cacti known as Turks head. There is much coastal erosion in this area and it is hard to imagine that this land once grew sugar and later cotton – only the ruins of a few old mills bear witness to its previous cultivation.

6 Round Hill From the summit of Round Hill (1014 feet) there are extensive and dramatic views looking towards Charlestown, across to the northern slope of Nevis Peak or over the Newcastle area and the airport. The road up to the summit was specially built for the erection of the radio mast. It provides an easy access to a most rewarding view point. Starting from either Cades Bay or Camps village drive up to the village of Fountain and from there follow the two-track road which is on the right of the Methodist church. Keep left at the end of the concrete then follow the road up the hillside – which becomes too steep for the average car to negotiate, so that the last half mile must be done on foot.

Other walks are to be found starting from various hotels. From Montpelier there is a walk to Cox Village or to Saddle Hill to find the old battery and Nelson's 'look-out' where on a clear day several of the neighbouring islands can be seen. From Zetlands and Old Manor Hotel there are walks along the hillside path to Rawlins and Stony Hill as well as a climb up the hill above Dunbar Mill onto the plateau. At the north end of the island there are walks close to Nisbet Plantation and Mount Nevis Hotel, such as the walk to Hogg Valley and Mount Pleasant, or to Camps Springs.

13 Flowers, fruits, trees and forests

The whole island of Nevis is a botanical garden, and much of its flora is to be seen along the roadsides: crotons, hibiscus, allamanda, plumbago, bougainvilleas, hybrid tea roses. All these grow in roadside gardens with many other trees and shrubs typical of the West Indies. Poinsettias bloom in the winter and spring as does the 'quick stick' with its showy pink flowers, the exotic immortel and the African tulip. Flamboyants flower in the summer months as well as bauhinias and frangipani. Mexican creeper grows as a weed, climbing and creeping everywhere; lantana grows without any encouragement. Cacti grow along the roadside, with species of aloes and sisal.

Fruits are in abundance: bananas, paw-paws (papaya), grapefruit, oranges, guavas, sour-sop, and avocado pears. A wide variety of tropical trees can be seen: silk cotton, calabash, white cedar, West Indian almond, casurina, sandbox (which has a trunk covered with sharp spines) and the turpentine or gum tree,

Allamanda

Yellowbelle

conspicuous because of its reddish-brown bark. Coconut trees grow all around the island, and the Royal palm or mountain cabbage palm (there are twelve varieties of Royal palm) grows on high ground.

Exotic plants are to be found in private gardens and hotel grounds. Montpelier has a beautiful garden with a large weeping fig tree at the entrance. The landscaping of the grounds and gardens at Four Seasons have won an award. There are numerous palms and stunning bougainvillea, to mention only a few specimens. A botanical garden has been developed which contains a rainforest conservatory and a tropical vine garden as well as an orchid terrace and an extensive collection of palms. A very old banyan tree can be seen at Morning Star – this used to be a traditional place for picnickers.

Beware the manchineel trees which border the seashore in various places. The round fruits are deadly poisonous and the milky sap is a strong irritant to the skin and eyes. Even handling the leaves can cause blistering. Despite the fact that so many new homes have been built up on the west-facing hillsides, there are still wild flowers to be found such as amaryllis (known locally as Easter lily), spider lilies, rain lilies which resemble crocuses, and black-eyed Susan. The Barbados cherry, a small, bright red fruit growing on an evergreen bush, is a delicious thirst quencher, whereas the fruits of the sea grape are not as delectable as they appear.

Almost twelve thousand acres of Nevis are covered with wood and forest. Above the 1000 foot contour line there is dense forest which is difficult to penetrate except in a few places. Below this line the majority of the trees are evergreen and include white cedar, laurels and various myrtles including the bay rum tree. The undergrowth is a mass of shrubs and vines, sprawling roots and ferns. Vanilla is to be found and species of epiphytic orchids. David Robinson and Jennifer Lowery have published an excellent description of the natural history of Nevis which includes an exhaustive list of trees and shrubs to be found at the various elevations. There is plenty to interest the botanist on Nevis.

Chenille ▷

14 Birds

There are about seventy different species of bird to be found on Nevis, about half of which are year-round residents. The red-tailed hawk and the American kestrel, known locally as the killy-killy, are both common and easy to identify. There are several types of doves and pigeons. Thrashers are seen frequently and the grey kingbird is often seen sitting on telephone wires or high tree tops. A trembler might be seen in the rainforest. Bananaquits and the redbreasted bullfinches can become tame to the point of being a nuisance around the house. A mocking bird is sometimes heard near citrus orchards; this large bird has a loud and melodious song. Several species of herons are present: the yellow-crowned heron, the small green heron and the blue heron. The last two birds prefer fresh water, which is also the habitat of the great egret, an entirely white, long-necked heron. The cattle egrets are to be seen pecking insects off the backs of cattle and sheep. Before sunset they fly in droves to roost in trees for the night. Brown pelicans are numerous around the coast, either gliding close to the surface of the water or diving into the sea

Contemplative pelican with the Narrows and St Kitts in the background

with a resulting large splash. Frigate birds look magnificent soaring above the sea and inland where they glide on the thermals. The tiny little birds which trip along the water's edge are sandpipers; terns also frequent the sea shores and occasionally willets have been seen in fresh water pools near Indian Castle. The hummingbirds are very small and exquisitely coloured; their plumage is iridescent although they appear almost black in the field. Because of their rapid and bee-like flight they are also called honey-bees. The species seen in Nevis is the purple-throated carib with its metallic green wings, the green-throated carib and the Antillean crested hummingbird. Their tiny nests are the size of a thimble and have been found in a candlestick!

⓵⑤ Creatures large and small

The largest wild animal to be found in Nevis is the monkey. When they were introduced, and how many there are, are both uncertainties, though the French have been blamed for bringing monkeys to St Kitts at some far distant date. The monkeys live in forest areas on the mountainsides and, as they help themselves to any available food crop ranging from peanuts to citrus fruits, they are a great nuisance to farmers. They are to be seen all over the island, sometimes leaping from branch to branch between tops of trees and over roof tops. They seem immune to any effort to reduce their number such as trapping.

Lizards are very common; several species can be identified but the green lizard – anolie – is seen everywhere on trees and climbing plants. Watch them as they change colour to match their background or when they inflate their throats, remaining motionless with their heads erect; a parent lizard carries its young under one back and one front leg, teaching it to climb vertical surfaces. The tiny gecko seen in the house serves a useful purpose by consuming insects.

There are large frogs and tiny frogs, and a large toad, a harmless creature to humans but hardly attractive. The tiny tree frog contributes to the nocturnal noises with its high-pitched, bell-like chirp. Another nocturnal creature is the land crab which was a useful source of food after being purged of poisonous matter and then fattened. The fire fly which emits a bright light from its abdomen is called a Simey Jimmy. Bats are seen at night – or in the day time if you venture into old buildings where a cluster of fruit bats might be found clinging upside down from a corner of the roof. Avoid the donkey spider, which can bite. Mongooses often dart across the roads; they were brought here a century ago to exterminate the rats which had inflicted great damage on the sugar cane.

Honey bees have been documented here as far back as 1716, brought from Europe by the early settlers. By tradition, honeycutting has been a source of income for a small number of intrepid farmers, who cut the honey from wild nests found around the island in hollow trees, old buildings, even abandoned vehicles. The cut honey is strained from the wax and put into old rum bottles for selling in the market. Since 1987 assistance has been given to encourage beekeeping in movable Langstroth beehives, a far more economical method; the liquid honey is sold and the beeswax made into candles or used in batique work. It is fascinating to watch the bees at work on various flowers and trees including coconut, mango, genip, lycidia coral creeper and hibiscus.

Butterflies are seen in profusion, especially after rain. *Nymphalidae* include the southern daggertail, the red rim, the malachite, the mimic, the painted lady and the Caribbean buckeye; from the *Heliconiidae*, the flambeau and the zebra are fairly common. *Pieridae* are the most common: tiny migrant sulphurs and the large orange-barred sulphur. Among the *Hesperiidae* are the tropical chequered skipper and the fiery skipper.

Green vervet monkey
(Cercopithecus sabaeus)

⑯ Agriculture and fishing

As the plantations fell into disuse the local population acquired parts of the cultivated land. The economic pattern of the island shifted towards small peasant farms which were marginally profitable. In the 1930s, when the depression on Nevis and elsewhere in the Caribbean was at its lowest ebb, the Government took over certain estates in an effort to stimulate agriculture. A considerable number of acres are still owned by the Government and there are full- and part-time farmers growing crops or keeping cattle. The food crops grown include yams, sweet potatoes, peanuts and vegetables such as cabbage, carrots, sweet peppers, tomatoes, pumpkins, beans, etc. Most of these are sold locally, some to the hotels. In parts of Gingerland, where some of the best soil is found, ginger, nutmeg and cinnamon are grown. The Department of Agriculture has developed a number of irrigation schemes to encourage farmers to produce vegetables throughout the year. Water is obtained mainly from surface run-off and is stored in large dams which can be seen at Spring Hill, at Potworks and above New River. A very useful tractor service is also provided to assist farmers with ploughing and ridging of land. Cotton is no longer grown, nor is there any sugar cane to be seen.

▲ Goats near New River

Coconut plantations were established at the beginning of the last century on the old sugar estates. Although badly damaged in recent hurricanes the palms still form an attractive feature of the island.

Livestock has always been an important part of agriculture on Nevis since the days when sugar estates produced their own working animals. Cattle, sheep, goats and poultry are kept by farmers who either own or rent land. The island is self-sufficient in eggs. The Government still owns land at Indian Castle where beef cattle can be seen grazing. The Veterinary Department is responsible for the control of tick diseases and has a tagging system for animals for identification purposes. An abattoir with full cold storage facilities and meat processing is in full use. Erosion has taken place over the island due to overgrazing and drought, which is not infrequent.

▲ The donkey was once an invaluable means of transport on Nevis

Clusters of fishing boats and accompanying tackle can be seen in bays around the coast, below Jessops, Long Haul Bay, Newcastle, Butlers, Indian Castle and Gallows Bay. About three hundred fishermen work more or less full time; their boats, which are made locally, have small outboard motors. Some of the fish are caught in pots through line fishing, others by nets and trawling methods. The main fish landed are lobster, bonito, snapper, kingfish and sometimes dolphin as well as smaller species. Competition with Japanese fishing vessels which are large and fast is leaving inadequate stocks for local boats.

The fishing co-operative provides cold storage for all fish. Turtles are also caught on occasions. They are rare, and a closed season has existed for them for several decades. Both these and lobsters are in danger of being overfished and having their existence placed in jeopardy. Deep sea fishing for visitors is available with experienced captains via Nevis Water Sports or Deep Venture.

▲ Fishing boats at Pinneys Beach

⑰ Cooking on Nevis

There is nothing monotonous about the food on Nevis. The restaurants and hotels offer a diverse number of dishes. Goat water is the best known; this stew is made from either goat or mutton and is served as a 'Saturday night special' and for any important event such as a wedding or a homecoming. 'Souce' is a similar stew but made with pork. All sorts of fish can be eaten; salt fish, which is a delicacy for some, is stewed with a spicy sauce. Dolphin, kingfish, snapper and grouper are generally baked; shark is fried or steamed with a lime and butter sauce. Conch is used for soup – 'conch chowder' – or included in a sauce to produce conch-stuffed lobster.

Hot pepper sauce is a speciality of Nevis. It can accompany any meat or fish dish. Creole sauce, which is served with chicken and fish dishes, is a blend of onions, sweet peppers, tomatoes, lime juice and seasonings. Locally grown vegetables are used with ingenuity: green papaya is transformed into a delicate soup as well as being served as a vegetable. Breadfruit is a substitute for white potatoes, pumpkins appear as soup, stuffed, made into fritters or used for dessert dishes. Tannia fritters, yam flan and 'callaloo' are all typical of Caribbean cookery. Sweet potatoes are boiled, baked, grilled or fried. Bananas, mangoes and coconuts, which all grow in abundance here, are used in countless ways; try mango ice cream, plantain puffs, coconut pie or banana flambé. Drinks are made from passion fruit, sour-sop, tamarind, ginger and guavas. At Christmas time the sorrel flowers are mixed with sugar, cloves and ginger to produce a traditional beverage. A one-pot meal, either a stew or a soup, is the main meal for most families: some meat or chicken wings, yams, sweet potatoes, pumpkin, cabbage, pigeon peas with the addition of

▶ Breadfruit grow in abundance

▲ Food on Nevis is varied and tasty

herbs and spices are the choice of ingredients which provide a nourishing dish. There are some good bakeries around the island which sell white and brown loaves as well as the traditional pork bread and coconut pies. All are delicious.

⑱ Culturama

This festival of folk art is held annually from the last Thursday in July until the first Monday in August. It originated from the efforts of the Nevis Drama and Cultural Society to retain the wealth of folklore which was slowly dying out. An exhibition is held for local artists who display pottery, paintings, crafts and woodwork including some well-made furniture. A vital part of Culturama is the calypso competition; the winner is declared 'Calypso King' and the winner of the Miss Culture competition is the 'Calypso Queen'. Troupes of masqueraders perform during the week; these traditional dancers have their roots in African folklore and the act has been handed down over centuries. Those taking part are dressed in gay and colourful costumes, including tall pointed hats adorned with peacock feathers. They dance to 'big drum music'. During the first ten years of Culturama money was raised towards a cultural centre at Grove Park which provides facilities for theatrical productions and concerts. Culturama has become a big event in the Caribbean. Not only Nevisians who work overseas but also people from other islands and from all walks of life come here for a 'piece of action'. They crowd the streets of Charlestown day and night and participate in a truly Nevisian occasion.

Gingerland's response to Culturama is to hold its own festival, Gingerama, at Christmas time, when music and drama are presented.

🔞 Music

Music is an important way of life to most West Indians and the people of Nevis are no exception. Bands play for evening entertainment or at barbecue lunches on the beaches, especially during the main tourist season. Interest in traditional music is growing. The Honey Bees were one of the earliest bands; their wind instruments which were all made locally included a fife, flute, banjo, guitar, mandolin and a quako (four-stringed guitar), a steel triangle and a horn made from the trunk of a tree called a baho. There are now several similar groups who perform, as well as string bands and steel pan groups. Steel pan music plays an important role on Nevis. The instrument is the only one that originated in the Caribbean, having been invented by a Trinidadian in 1947. Leroy Parris is an extremely talented pan player who performs at various places around the island and who has shared his talent with both young and old.

At Christmas time there is some fine singing by church choirs who visit private houses as well as hotels to sing carols. Once or twice a year combined choirs give a concert which is well worth hearing.

Playing a home-made string bass at ▶
Oualie Beach Hotel

⑳ Crafts and paintings

There is a considerable amount of craftwork produced on Nevis: pottery from local clay, baskets from screw pine, mats made from kush-kush grass, carvings and furniture from local woods. In the Nevis Craft House, situated in the old Cotton Ginnery, a wide variety of goods are for sale made by members of the handicraft co-operative which was started over twenty years ago in an effort to assist people with a craft to market their products as well as giving training for members. In Walwyn Square the Nevis Co-op sells home made food as well as clothing and mats. Cane work from the workshop for the blind is also on sale.

At the top of Zion Hill, Kennedy, a deaf and dumb man sits outside his home carving models of animals. He has had the minimum of training and has put his ideas into his creative work. Furniture is made on a small scale but with a high standard of craftsmanship and is to be found at various workshops around the island.

The Nevis Pottery is near Newcastle; the range of items sold includes jugs, ashtrays, baking pots (as used on Nevis since time immemorial), models of St James' church, candle covers and plant pots – to mention only a few of their wares. The technique used here has been handed down over generations of potters who have lived in this area. The clay soil comes from Potworks, and the

unique red colour of the finished pots comes from a local rock which has to be crushed to produce the shiny finish. Firing takes

place in an open fire of coconut shells. There are about twelve potters who can be seen at work, moulding, painting, mixing or firing.

An increasing number of artists exhibit and sell their works. A collection of the late Eva Wilkin's original paintings and prints are on sale in the Gallery at Clay Ghaut Mill. This is where Eva lived for many years, painting scenes of her life around her as well as people. In Charlestown the Gallery of Art has pictures by Marie Clarke and Margaret Fraser as well as attractive painted furniture. In the Café des Arts, next to the

Museum of Nevis, work by the sculptor Robert Humphreys can be seen, as well as work by Mr Chapman, a local stone sculptor. There are prints of Dorothy Cleary's scenes of Nevis which are well known for their charm; Alvin Grant's pictures are also of great merit. Other local artists display their paintings and crafts during Culturama week.

▲ Potters at work in the Nevis Pottery, Newcastle

The Eva Wilkin ▶ Gallery, in a converted sugar mill at Clay Ghaut

㉑ Cricket and sport

Nevisians have always been fanatical about cricket; everyone knows about the finer points of the game, everyone is willing to talk about cricket, to watch cricket and to listen to cricket matches on the radio whether they are at work or at home. Any group of boys is happy to play a game on the beach using the stem of a coconut branch as a stump, a home-made bat and an old tennis ball. There is an island team as well as village teams and school teams. Nevis has been playing in the Leeward Islands Tournament since 1941; the first Leeward Islander to play for the West Indies against Australia was Nevisian Elquimedo Tonito Willet, a left-arm spinner who toured England in the West Indies team in 1973. Keith Arthurton is regarded with great respect, being a formidable left-handed all rounder. Anyone with an enthusiasm for cricket should watch a game at Grove Park; the Shell Shield competition is played in February and the Leeward Islands tournament in June.

▲ A serious business – the passion for cricket is everywhere

Football (soccer) comes next in popularity to cricket and is played around the island. The Nevis Football Association organises competitions which are sponsored by the St Kitts Breweries Ltd. The netball season starts at the beginning of May; five teams compete against each other and the Nevis team participates in the Caribbean Netball Association matches. There are tennis courts at most of the hotels where non-residents are welcomed. In Charlestown a generous donor has provided courts for the use of schools and the general public.

Horse racing has resumed its popularity again – it is a big tourist attraction and has a loyal following. The Nevis Turf and Jockey Club, a voluntary organisation, laid out a new track at Indian Castle with parade ring and grandstand. There are twelve meets a year, the

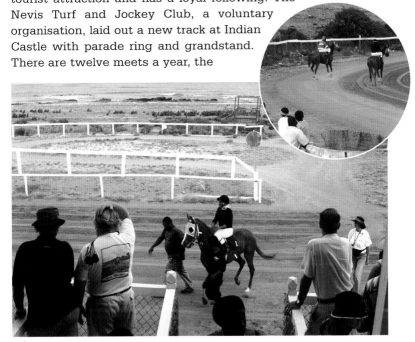

▲ Horse racing

popular ones being on Boxing Day, Easter Monday and during Culturama week.

An 18-hole golf course was constructed in 1990 as part of the Four Seasons Hotel complex. It is a spectacular course which non-residents of the hotel are welcome to use at certain times. The popularity of this course means that golf enthusiasts come to the island specifically to play on the course. There are also two other courses, the original one-hole course near Jones Bay as well as one up Shaws Road. There are cycle tracks around the island and several equestrian centres for horse riders.

㉒ Stamps

Nevis has the distinction of having been the first of the Leeward Islands to produce its own postage stamp when in 1861 the Nevis Council and Assembly took over the postal arrangements from the Colonial Government. The design of the stamp was a facsimile of the Great Seal of the Colony which depicted a scene at the Bath Springs. The series was issued in values of one penny, four pence, six pence and one shilling in sheets of twelve stamps each. The shilling stamps of the 1861 and the 1867 issues are both extremely valuable as they are very rare. In 1879 Nevis joined the Postal Union and later used the general design of the Leeward Isles, which was the head of the reigning monarch, Queen Victoria. By joining the Postal Union the cost of postage for letters to the UK or the USA was reduced from one shilling to one penny. After 1903 the stamps issued were for St Kitts-Nevis and several stamps of historical interest were produced, such as the issue in 1923 to celebrate the third centenary of the founding of the Colony of St Kitts.

After nearly one hundred years Nevis started to issue her own stamps again and has produced some of the most attractive stamps in the Caribbean area. Since 1980 there have been four or five issues each year. Included in the series are the butterflies of Nevis, the corals and birds of Nevis, local scenes, Culturama and

First Day Cover celebrating the work of Eva Wilkin

boats as well as international events such as Commonwealth Day, the Royal Weddings, the birth of Prince William, etc. School children were invited to submit designs for the Christmas 1982 issue and the design for the first anniversary of Independence was chosen from competition entries submitted by Nationals.

Stamps and first day covers can be purchased at the Philatelic Bureau as well as enlargements of certain stamps made into unusual postcards. Standing orders for future issues of stamps can also be made so that visitors from overseas may be supplied and become collectors of these commemorative issues.

㉓ Facts and figures

POPULATION
The population of Nevis in 2003 was 10 000. 50% are under fifteen years of age and 11% are over sixty. Emigration to the United States of America is minimal and there are a number of returning immigrants. In addition small numbers of people have come from other places in the Caribbean such as Guyana and Trinidad.

EMPLOYMENT
The biggest employers of labour are the government departments, hotels and restaurants. Other employers include construction companies, shops, banks, commercial firms, light industries, motor mechanics and domestic workers. Minimum wages are stipulated for most categories of labour.

EDUCATION
The Medical College of the Americas has built a medical school at Potworks where students from many parts of the world receive training for a medical degree. The University of the West Indies has a Distance Learning Centre in Charlestown. There are six primary schools, two secondary schools and a sixth form college which are all provided by the state. There are also three private schools covering ages from pre-school to age sixteen.

ORGANISATIONS
Nevis has a small defence force which receives regular training. The two main political parties are the Nevis Reform Party (NRP) and the Concerned Citizen Movement who hold power at present in the Nevis Island Assembly. Various other organisations include a gardening club and the Alexander Hospital Auxiliary Society which provides comforts for hospital patients. The Red Cross and the Lions Club have meetings, as well as other organisations such as the Nevis Animal Rescue and Care.

HEALTH
Alexander Hospital in Government Road has been rebuilt during the last decade. It provides a general hospital service including a maternity ward and a limited amount of surgery.

The primary health care of the community is the responsibility of the six health centres across the island. They are open five days a week and staffed with a variety of health workers, district midwives, family planning staff and district nurses. Child welfare, ante- and post-natal clinics are held, immunisations given, and family planning is available. A dental health assistant works full-time with school children and the health centre staff visit schools to give talks on health as well as carrying out immunisations. Casualties are treated daily and home visits are made to mentally and physically disadvantaged people who are cared for within the community rather than in an institution.

The public health department has an assortment of duties connected with sanitation, port health, inspection of premises, spraying mosquitoes, waste disposal, meat inspection and infectious diseases control.

WATER

Most of the piped water supplied for domestic use comes from the three main springs: the Nevis Peak source, Camp Springs and Maddens Springs, together with water pumped from boreholes at New River, Maddens and Bath Village. The water is stored in reservoirs fed by gravity or pumped to different areas. Charlestown has a piped water supply that has recently been completely renewed and all villages now have piped water. Hotels and private houses have in most cases built cisterns to store rain water from the roof. The average annual rainfall is 49 inches; the falls are usually slight – generally less than one inch per day. Heavy storms are rare. The last six months of the year have more rain than the first six months, when droughts can occur lasting two to three months. The west side of the island has a higher rainfall than the east side at the same altitude. Above 2000 feet the rainfall is significantly higher throughout the year.

RADIO AND TELEVISION

There are several radio stations including Radio Paradise and VON (Voice of Nevis). Local information and announcements are broadcast early in the morning and in the evenings, including weather forecasts and warnings of hurricanes. Many homes have cable television.

TRANSPORT

Roads

The original roads on the island existed for the transport of sugar from the plantations to the ports of Charlestown and St George. The present island road is 26 miles long; most of this has been upgraded and realigned. A road to link the deep water harbour to the north side of Charlestown avoiding the town centre is now completed.

A rural roads project, paid for by the European Development Fund, is repairing old roads as well as making new roads in areas which were previously isolated and remote.

Taxis are to be found at the airport and in Charlestown and there are several car rental firms. Privately owned minibuses run on the main road to convey passengers to Charlestown.

Sea

There are two ferries which run a regular service between St Kitts and Nevis – the *Carib Queen* and the *Carib Breeze*. The *Sea Hustler* runs between the Four Seasons Hotel and St Kitts.

▲ Ferry to St Kitts

Air

Newcastle airstrip is able to land 42- and 50-seater aircraft. A new airport building was completed in 2003. St Kitts and Antigua are both international airports but regional airlines such as LIAT and WINAIR and three charter air companies convey passengers to Nevis.

BANKS

There are five banks – the locally owned Bank of Nevis, the First Caribbean (Barclays), the Bank of Nova Scotia, the National Bank and the Royal Bank of Trinidad and Tobago. The currency is the East Caribbean Dollar which links to the US dollar at an exchange rate of roughly EC$2.69 to US$1.00.

TOURISM

The office of the Department of Tourism in the centre of Charlestown provides all necessary information regarding hotels, guest houses, rentals, real estate, ferry services, car hire, etc.

A plaque which hangs in the Museum of Nevis History commemorates the landing of the Virginian settlers in 1601. They stayed only six days. Some people come to Nevis for a one day visit, the majority stay longer, many have built homes here to spend winter on the island. Since independence the island has changed considerably. It is now tourism orientated. Poverty still exists but is hardly evident. The financial position has improved through investments, offshore banks, taxation and other forms of revenues as well as very generous grants from different sources. There is a unique quality about Nevis: it is friendly, simple and informal. It is an island for the discerning – it is indeed 'Queen of the Caribbees'.

Website and email address of Tourism Bureau
www.nevisisland.com
nta2001@caribsurf.com

Bibliography

Gertrude Atherton: *The Conqueror*

Gertrude Atherton: *The Gorgeous Isle*

Carl and Roberto Bridenbaugh: *No Peace beyond the Line*

Carl and Roberto Bridenbaugh: *The English in the Caribbean, 1624–1690*

Mrs Burdon: *Guide to St Kitts and Nevis 1920*

E. Byron: *Families of Nevis*

A. Coldecolt: *The Church in the West Indies*

Henry Nelson Coleridge, MA: *Six months in the West Indies in 1825*

Harry Edgington: *Nelson, the Hero and the Lover*

Elsa V. Goveia: *Slave Society in the British Leeward Islands at the end of the 18th Century*

J. Gordon: *The Little Duchess: The Story of Lord Nelson's Wife*

R. Greenwood and S. Hamber: *Arawaks to Africans*

R. Greenwood and S. Hamber: *Emancipation to Emigration*

R. Greenwood and S. Hamber: *Development and Decolonisation*

Paul Hilder: *The Birds of Nevis*

Vincent K. Hubbard: *Swords, Ships and Sugar (The History of Nevis)*

Patrick Leigh Fermour: *The Traveller's Tree*

Kathleen Manchester: *Historic Heritage of St Kitts-Nevis-Anguilla*

P.L. Matheson OBE: *The Thomas Warner Story*

Gordon C. Merrill: *The Historical Geography of St Kitts and Nevis*

Sir Harold Mitchell: *Europe in the Caribbean*

Fred Olsen: *On the Trail of the Arawaks*

Professor R. Pares: *A West Indian Fortune*

J.H. Parry and Philip Sherlock: *A Short History of the West Indies*

Paton: *Voyage to the Caribees: Down the Island*

Robert Southey: *The Life of Horatio, Lord Nelson*

C.M. Trevelyan: *English Social History*

Cannon G. Walker: *Cottle Church*

Alec Waugh: *A Family of Islands*

Eric Williams: *From Columbus to Castro*

Also available in the MACMILLAN CARIBBEAN GUIDES SERIES

Anguilla: Tranquil Isle of the Caribbean – Brenda Carty and Colville Petty

Antigua and Barbuda: Heart of the Caribbean – Brian Dyde

The Bahamas: Family of Islands – Gail Saunders

Barbados: The Visitors' Guide – F A Hoyos

Belize: Ecotourism in Action – Meb Cutlack

The Islands of Bermuda: Another World – David Raine

Dominica: Isle of Adventure – Lennox Honychurch

Dominican Republic: An Introduction and Guide – James Ferguson

Grenada: Isle of Spice – Norma Sinclair

Jamaica: The Fairest Isle – Philip Sherlock and Barbara Preston

St Kitts: Cradle of the Caribbean – Brian Dyde

St Lucia: Helen of the West Indies – Guy Ellis

St Vincent and the Grenadines – Lesley Sutty

Tobago: An Introduction and Guide – Eaulin Blondel

The Turks and Caicos Islands: Lands of Discovery – Amelia Smithers and Anthony Taylor

Other related titles from Macmillan Caribbean

Out of the Crowded Vagueness: A History of the islands of St Kitts, Nevis and Anguila – Brian Dyde

A History of St Kitts: The Sweet Trade – Vincent K Hubbard

Searching for Sugar Mills: An Architectural Guide to the Eastern Caribbean – Suzanne Gordon and Anne Hersh